CYCLES:

A Scientific Key to the Integration of the Metaphysical Disciplines

By

John Lawrence Maerz

© *John Lawrence Maerz 2009*

All Rights Reserved

ISBN 978-0-557-27153-5

Table of Contents

Introduction 7

Part 1

What is a Cycle? 9

Seasons & the Ancients: Cycles of Birth & Decay 11

THE PAGAN HOLIDAYS: Human Traditions for Change 13

Sowing and Reaping 16

THE I CHING: The Interplay of Polarity 18

LUNAR PHASES: The Blueprint for the Physical Universe 30

Joe's New Apartment 35

Uranus: The Life Clock 38

Saturn: The Tangible Clock 48

The Progressed Moon: The Internal Perceiver 48

Numerology and the Sub-Cycles 49

Who's Leading the Dance? The Timing and Interplay 51

The Cyclic Pattern in 3.5 Year Segments 52

Waxing Phases 53

Wanning Phases 57

Part II

How to Use This Section 64

CYCLE I: Learning

00-3.5   Emergence 67

3.5-7.0 Assertion 70

7.0-10.5 Action 72

10.5-14 Expression 73
14-17.5 Fulfillment 75
17.5-21 Synthesis 76
21-24.5 Reorientation 77
24.5-28 Release 79

CYCLE II: Production
28-31.5 Emergence 81
31.5-35 Assertion 82
35-38.5 Action 84
38.5-42 Expression 85
42-45.5 Fulfillment 86
45.5-49 Synthesis 90
49-52.5 Reorientation 91
52.5-56 Release 93

CYCLE III: Establishing Balance
56-59.5 Emergence 96
59.5-63 Assertion 97
63-66.5 Action 98
66.5-70 Expression 99
70-73.5 Fulfillment 101
73.5-77 Synthesis 102
77-80.5 Reorientation 104
80.5-84 Release 106

CYCLE IV: Another Dance?

84-87.5 Emergence   108

Part III

45 Degree Chart   110

Recommended Reading   112

About the Author   113

Other Books by
John Lawrence Maerz

TAROT: The Astrological Layout
A Comprehensive Guide for Integrating Astrology, Tarot & Numerology

IS ANYONE THERE?
Learning to Reach Across the Veil in Mediumship

INTRODUCTION

In nature a river is a symbol of life. It moves following the natural laws of gravity and motion. There are times when it swells and times when it contracts but as long as there is water there will be *some* kind of movement. A leaf falling into the water will float for a while and move with the current. It will flow through bends and dips and over water falls. When the water slows the leaf will slow. It will passively move to wherever the water moves. When *we* fall into the water and if we remain completely relaxed and passive we will follow the same pattern of travel. However, humans are not known for being relaxed and passive. Most likely our brains will look to find the closest bank and attempt to swim towards it. Some of us will even be stupid enough to swim against the current toward where we fell from. The same circumstance occurs at the beach when we are swept away by a rip tide. Our natural instinct is to swim against the current to get back to shore. If we just relax and let the current carry us a little bit out of our way we could easily swim back by a different route and maybe even *with* the current. Life is exactly the same. Despite the fact that we feel the currents, we still consistently find ourselves swimming *against* the current because we don't understand the dynamics of how energy flows in the natural cycle. Had we understood the natural pattern of flow we could easily anticipate variations and move with the flow. This book attempts to do just that; recognize the pattern of flow in the natural cycle of our lives so we may be prepared for shifts and have a clearer understanding of what might come next.

Over the years and through the many disciplines I have investigated I have come to understand that there are many traditions that expose the natural patterns of nature through their practices. The ancients knew much more through observing nature than our scientific academia will care to admit. Yet, we still put our faith in things like allopathic medicine which fixes the symptoms and the barn door after the horses have gone when an ounce of prevention could have eliminated the potential for problems in the first place. But prevention requires patient observation of how energy moves through our world. We have lost that patience and hence, lost the ability to work *with* the natural flow of things. Our culture has a stubborn desire to "make a difference" in everyday life though pushing the stone up the hill much like Sisyphus did.

In this book I present an opportunity to see the natural cycle of life and energy, as I have, moving through four different traditions. These are, essentially, four different languages for perceiving the same action in the world. There are many more traditions that embrace the natural flow in their teachings. I invite you to look into your own traditions and observations and see if you can perceive the same permeating patterns of the cycle.

-John Maerz

Part 1
WHAT IS A CYCLE?

The old statement, "What goes around, comes around" is a lot truer than one might think. Contrary to how movement might appear to the naked eye, all energy travels in circles or cycles. Cycle comes from Lower Latin as *cyclus* and Greek as *kyklos*. Random House unabridged dictionary describes a cycle as any complete round or series of occurrences that repeats or is 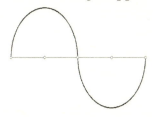 repeated. In the diagram to the right you'll notice a circle opened to produce a mathematical representation in a pictorial form that scientists call a sine wave. Pictured here is a single cycle. This is the graphic and most common way to show the cycle where changes or values may be illustrated. If we add the same picture end to end a

 number of times we will see a picture of what we refer to as a wave. The wave is the basic form that energy, in any application, takes when moving through time and space. You'll notice, in the third diagram, that what is repeated in a cycle is, basically, an "on" and "off" state much like a light switch in a dark room. When we enter a room and flip the switch to power a light it appears as if the light is on immediately. If we were to slow time we would see that it grows in brightness, gradually, to a peak luminescence and it dims, just as gradually, when flipped off. This is illustrated in the diagram as it moves up or down with the gradually changing wave. On various points along the wave, the brightness or dimness is shown by the height of the 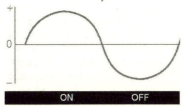 wave. In the same way, daylight changes into night and night changes into daylight gradually. This is due to the fact that the Earth rotates once every twenty four hours returning to its original starting point

completing one cycle of repetition. There are no sharp or definite divisions between the two states; light or dark and on or off. It is our mind that regards a cycle in such a fashion so we have a static representation to compare the opposing states. Our mind arranges things in a system of polarities so it can have a point of reference and "see" a definitive linear change. In reality, all change is gradual and it is our mind that simplifies it for its own understanding. All cycles, eventually, return to the beginning point at the completion of each cycle. Let's expand this concept further.

Imagine attaching a string to a ball and swinging it around your head. In the process of swinging there is a point when it is directly in front of you, directly to your left, directly behind you, directly to your right and, again, directly in front of you. We divide the cycle in divisions our mind can understand. Just like we can divide the cycle into four equal quadrants and have north, south, east and west we can still divide the cycle further into eight equal points of the compass; N, NNE, E, SSE, S, SSW, W, NNW. We can *still* take our division further to *ad infinitum* to any number of divisible sections. Think of cutting a pizza. Whether you slice it into six pieces or eight pieces the amount and quality of the pizza remains the same.

The most common scientific division of a circle or cycle is 360 parts or degrees and even that can be divided still further into minutes and seconds. If we divide our pizza into twelve equal parts we will end up with twelve equal thirty degree segments as used in astrology. As

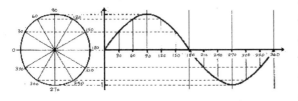

in the diagram to the left, each sign or thirty degree segment will represent a different magnetic potential or point of development on the curve in the repetition of the cycle. So every time the "ball on a string" comes back to the same point or direction within the swing we can see and feel the same tension that was exhibited at the same point in the last cycle and predict the same tension in future cycles. Hence, we now have a consistent and reliable pattern that we can rely on and every time the cycle comes back to the same point we know we will feel and sense it the same way. Let's move on, now that we have an understanding of how a cycle operates, to seeing cycles in nature and philosophy.

THE SEASONS & THE ANCIENTS:
UNDERSTANDING THE CYCLE OF BIRTH AND DECAY

The Earth revolves around the Sun once every 365.25 days. At the same time the Earth leans on its axis and because of this leaning the angle of the sun's rays touching the Earth varies throughout the year. Within this cycle there are times when the light is more intense at some times of the year and less at others. The winter solstice, December 21st, is the time that the sun's rays are at the most oblique angle conveying the least heat. The summer solstice, June 21st, is the time when the sun's rays are the most direct and, consequently, the most intense heat. The spring and fall equinoxes, March 21st and September 21st, are when this heat and light are balanced exactly between the both intensities. In the diagram to the right you'll notice that the year is divided by four into, roughly, three months or ninety days for each season. If we start with summer the intensity of the light is the 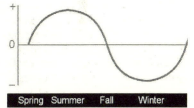 highest in amplitude or height on our pictorial wave. The winter is where it is the lowest. The spring and fall are where they are equal to each other at the midpoint. This represents the basic planting cycle our ancestors followed. In the winter, when the amplitude of light is the lowest vegetation is at seed, moving into gestation, in the deepest part of the earth. At spring it births up past the horizon or surface level showing early growth. At summer it is the highest in amplitude and vegetation has grown to the highest and most visible state. At fall it reduces in intensity as we harvest the fruits released. At winter the heat and light reduce further as the vegetation releases even its leaves retreating back into the earth to serve as nutrition for the seed it has dropped. And then we start the cycle again. The ancient Celts divided the year, further, into eight parts. Each quarter year was halved again to approximately forty five days each. These four new dates correspond, approximately, to February 1st, May 1st, August 1st and November 1st. Starting with the winter solstice the holidays (Holy days) are called Yule, Imbolc, Esotar, Beltane, Litha, Lugnasad, Mabon and Samhain. This brings us to the eight phase cycle which appears to be the temporal framework for many world disciplines, religions and philosophies. Let's move on to describing eight phase cycle in its earliest appearance.

THE PAGAN HOLIDAYS:
HUMAN TRADITIONS FOR CHANGE

One of the oldest western European cultures was the Druids. We know very little of them. We assume that their legacy and history was absorbed by the Celts who are credited with showing some of the first tangible patterns for working with the agrarian yearly cycle in the form of a holiday "schedule" that we still follow today. The holidays that follow are considered pagan since they follow and signify times in the natural yearly cycle for planting and reaping. Over time, as Christianity was adopted over pagan patterns, the names of the holidays changed and took on a Christian flavor but the underlying principles for importance remained the same. They now represented events in the Christian tradition that coincided with the natural cycle.

The solstices and equinoxes change with the Sun's movement through the zodiac. As the winter solstice begins on or about December 21st the exact timing is when the Sun moves into the first degrees of Capricorn. The diagram to the left will show this movement. Please note that for simplicity's sake I will begin our cycle, from here on in, at the top of each diagram and move in a counterclockwise direction for the rest of this book. I do this since, in the natural astrology chart, Capricorn begins on the top of the chart and progresses through the signs in a counterclockwise direction. I

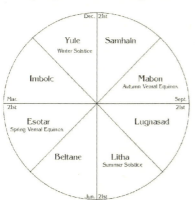

will do this with the other sections in this book in an endeavor to keep the conceptual template consistent for easy reference.

Before I start going through the holidays you should understand that the pagan system is one where there are two balancing and interchanging forces that create their dynamic world. There is the Goddess which is symbolic of all things earthbound, material and receptive and there is the God which is symbolic of all things heaven bound, spiritual and active. This should NOT be taken as representative of our cultural "battle of the sexes" that permeates all of our social interplay. Neither entity is superior or inferior. Both are equally important.

YULE: This is the winter solstice. This time represents the birth of the king to the Goddess. In zodiacal terms, it is the rebirth of the Sun. It is the shortest day of the year with the greatest darkness thereby marking the beginning of increasing daylight. The underlying principle is that the ultimate product of death is rebirth. In agrarian terms the seed is at its deepest in the earth and it exhibits the least amount of external activity. It is passing out of dormancy. It represents a time of unlimited possibilities since there is no visible pattern or template for life to follow. For the Romans this is the celebration of Saturnalia and for the Christians this is the birth of the Christ.

IMBOLC: This holiday is also known as Brigid's Day, Candlemas, Cross Quarter Day, the Feast of Pan, Festival of Light and Lupercalia. This is the time of recovery for the Goddess after the king's birth. It is also a beginning where the earth, warmed by the sun's rays, germinates and sprouts the new seedlings. In the Christian tradition, this is the time Mary presents the child king to the temple or Hypapante and begins her forty day process of purification. Also, at this time, candles are blessed for use throughout the year.

OSTARA: This holiday is also known as Eostar, Ishtar, Astarte, Esotar and Easter. This is the vernal equinox where the length of daylight is equal to, and then overtakes, darkness. It's a time of fertility and rebirth. This is the time where the sprouted seedling burst through the surface and begin a period of voracious growth. Internal energy and external movement are equal to each other. In the Christian tradition this is the resurrection of the Christ figure.

BELTANE: This is May Day and Cross Quarter Day. This is the marriage of the God and the Goddess. This is, traditionally, the time of pagan hand fasting (modern day preference for June weddings). It is a time of conception. The child king has grown into manhood and impregnates the Goddess. The maypole and the cauldron are the reflective symbols of phallic power. In agrarian terms this is the period that anything growing morphs into its own particular uniqueness as a plant. It explodes from a seedling and a small plant struggling for survival to channeling tremendous energy into growth into its own, one of a kind, individuality.

LITHA: This is the summer solstice. This is the longest day of the year. The Sun is the highest and the brightest it will be for the rest of the year. Pagans leap across the bonfires (Sun) to promote fertility in animals and crops. The placenta begins to grow within the Goddess. This is also the time that nature is the most fully visible. Everything has bloomed to its fullest splendor. New growth has reached its highest potential. Nature is the most open and vital through its flowers and blooms. Now begins the time of taking all this energy in growth and transforming it into fruit. At this point darkness begins to gradually move toward dominance and the focus and movement of the cycle changes from creating to letting go.

LUGHNASAD: This is also referred to as Lammas, the Feast of Bread, August Eve and Cross Quarter day. This is the time of the first harvest and the first release of fruit to the ground to nourish the forest inhabitants. This is the year's largest and most visible release of nurturance.

MABON: This is the autumn equinox. Day and night are equal in length. The journey inward begins. Building a nest and gathering fruit to survive the winter becomes the drive. This is the second harvest. The leaves turn and begin to fall to allow more sunlight to reach the ground to warm the seeds that have fallen thus far.

SAMHAIN: This is also November Eve, Feast of the Dead, Cross Quarter Day and All Hallows Eve. This is a time of sacrifice. This is the last harvest and the last opportunity to store nurturance to carry us through the winter. The last cover of the forest falls and the veil between the living and the dead becomes the thinnest. The forest is fully mulched to protect the fallen seedlings throughout the winter.

SOWING & REAPING

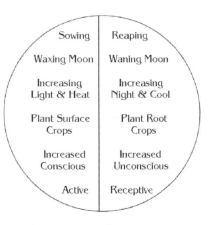

If you'll look back to the preceding eight holidays you will notice that the first four are generative or active and the last four are "passive" or receptive. In any cycle there is the building of energy and then its retreat. This is also true of the yearly cycle whether we label it pagan style or otherwise. This is the idea behind Karma where the statement is, "Whatever goes around comes around." The principle is that whatever energy that is set in motion must resolve or rebalance itself. This may take more than one cycle but will eventually rebalance since it constantly seeks to do so until it is. This can happen in a minute, a day, a year, a lifetime or through many lifetimes. It doesn't need our recognition to be effective and the "debt" or imbalance registers with the universe as an out of sync energy needing to be resolved. Think of a pendulum that's set in motion in one direction. The natural inclination is to return to a balanced state. It will remain in that "charged" or imbalanced state with full magnetic pull until the opportunity presents itself where it can "discharge." The same is true of Karma. From a human perspective, whatever we have set in motion we must witness and experience the complimentary energy whether they are "acts of random kindness" or the worst kind of atrocity. Our awareness or unawareness of this potential is not necessary for the universe to do what it is polarized to do. It is "mindless" or, more appropriately, the universe is without intent that can be understood within our comprehension. It simply is. Therefore, there is no moral component to Karma except that it rebalances itself, hence, no conscience or guilt. This is universal law.

In any event, literally, what is to be understood is that a cycle will represent both parts of any energetic movement; a chosen action (sowing) and a corresponding resolution (reaping) or return to its original state. To understand this will, at best, remind us that there are consequences to EVERY action (*con* = with and *sequence* = order). This understanding will be of tremendous use when we investigate predictive astrology utilizing planetary cycles. We can see this understanding very clearly in another discipline; I Ching. Let's push on.

THE I CHING:
THE INTERPLAY OF POLARITY

From an eastern perspective the Orientals follow and promote the same understanding of action/reaction through the familiar Yin and Yang. Yin and Yang are points, in all concepts, of the extreme limits of any polarity. In this fashion we need white to identify black and black to identify white. Up and down are needed to identify each other. Hot and cold are needed to identify each other. Yet, neither extreme exists without a small portion of the other existing within the opposing polarity. So, all facets of existence exist in varying degrees between each of the opposing, extreme polarities. For the westerner, the extremes, or the "blacks and whites of it," are easy for us to understand. We, the westerners, label everything in what we the easterner would see as a static picture. But when it comes to the varying degrees of existence between these static identities, or labels, we have immense difficulty identifying and accepting their gradual changes. To us, grey, and variations of grey, are not acceptable for us to use in our reasoning. Our logic requires "solid" points of reference to operate. To wit, our science is based on "facts" or static points of identity agreed upon by the scientific community. To get philosophical, a concept's "factuality" only exists if it is agreed upon by the group that sets the rules; in this case, the scientists.

To identify points of reference within the cycle the Chinese, first, divide the cycle into four which corresponds to the seasons. Second, they divide the cycle by eight. These are the Trigrams, which, we will explore. Third, they take this division further by dividing those eight by eight again yielding the sixty four points they refer to as Hexagrams. All of these divisions follow a prescribed order that shows a specific degree of change between each point. This gives them, and us, a way to identify those grey points between the extremes. This does a lot to identify a structure or organization that the material, logical mind can manipulate. For us westerners, to accept anyone or anything we need to be able to label them. Then we feel we are secure. Our mind has "control."

The Trigrams, as they are called, follow, essentially, the same pattern as the pagan holidays. As the holidays do, they always follow each other in the same order. The only variation you should be aware of, however, is that there are two manifestations of them in Chinese history. The first version is a theoretical or, if I can say relative to Chinese philosophy, a "spiritual" reflection they term "Earlier Heaven." They were set down by the first of the mythical Three Sovereigns, Fu Hsi in 2850BC. The second rendition has a more usable or mundane quality they term "Later Heaven." To research these you would explore the Trigrams as set down by King Wen of Zhou, 12th century BC. There is a whole mythology and mystic perspective behind these which I won't go into here but the I Ching, itself, can be a lifetime study which will never be fully comprehended by any individual in one lifetime. However, it is certainly worth any time and effort put into it. Now, let's move on to the Trigrams themselves and their characterizations of each of the eight segments. As with the pagan holidays we will begin with the winter and the top segment to the left of center. Please note that the order of the Trigrams is, traditionally, the same but that the "wheel" has been flipped to fit our western, eightfold template. (the west moves counterclockwise, the east clockwise)

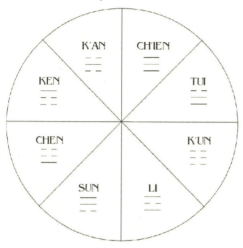

Each Trigram is consistent of three lines. The lines will be either of a Yin or Yang quality. A broken line represents the Yin or receptive quality and a solid line represents the Yang or active quality. The symbols I've included in each of the Trigrams exhibit qualities that will enhance our understanding of each part of the cycle as having a very different flavor. Watching each of the animals listed will give us a very subtle and integrated feel for how the energy presents itself. It should also be noted that T'ai Chi Ch'uan, which is an ancient oriental moving meditation, utilizes a mix of the movements and behaviors of many animals to produce a disciplined exercise that can aid us in aligning ourselves with our true animal natures. The Feng Shui aspects give us a feel of when, in the cycle, we will be able to utilize the most support while investing in specific activities. Please also note that the family positions, which do give a very useful portrayal of family dynamics, are in relation to a patriarchal family structure. In this light they will follow a more traditional line of expected family behaviors. To adjust these to a more contemporary reflection of family dynamics make require a deeper scrutiny.

As a beginning note, when we put two Trigrams together they make what's called a Hexagram of which there are sixty four in the I Ching or Book of Change. Each of the sixty four Hexagrams has its own interpretation and implication of how to use the energy in its part of the cycle. Each of the following Trigrams when doubled themselves, constitute eight of the possible sixty four. Each of these eight has an, overall, important meaning in its own right and can be considered an important mile stone in the scheme of the cycle. Let's proceed to delineate the eight.

K'AN – relates to *Water*. It encompasses the mysterious, the profound, meaningful, dangerous, difficult and abysmal. Its characteristic animal is the *Pig* representing domesticity. This period of the year begins on the winter solstice. Its personality is *Abysmal* and its family position is the *Middle Son*. In Feng Shui the aspect of life is *Career*.

Beginning any new endeavor, as this part of the cycle indicates, is a very delicate and tender time. Since the endeavor is new, there are no past patterns or guidelines in which to follow. In the I Ching the trigram portrayed is doubled to produce symbol 29, water over water, which is called "Danger." As water penetrates and permeates everything, the danger comes in where there are no boundaries to recognize or use to make decisions. There is nothing external. The listening must be done internally. Consider the *Middle Son*. There is no sense of belonging for him. He usually gets "lost in the shuffle." In a conventional family the eldest has the most expectations put on him and the youngest is the most contentious by rebelling against those expectations. You might say that the *Middle Son* gets the least amount of attention from the family. Essentially, he feels overlooked. If he's looking for outside approval or guidance he's "up the creek." But what he doesn't realize is that since there are so few expectations of him, he has the most freedom for choice in action. If he follows the "internal rudder" he will find tremendous success. Relative to the Pig, there is always a sense of lack and tendency toward acquiring more than what is necessary. He doesn't understand why but he feels that he can't help himself in "taking" or "being a pig" about things. Outside success, no matter how it comes, is never enough since the recognition he seeks does not come from the family unit from where he needs it. It should also be noted that a *Career* can be considered a "calling." This "calling" is always something that is registered on our internal sense of identity as a result of life experiences that feel like a hint or urge in a particular direction of endeavor. Again, the importance here is that it is internal.

So we can say that in any beginning endeavor the indications for direction and action must all come from our internal listening. That little voice inside is the only place where we can gain some help or understanding as to how to proceed. If we are learning to be self motivated or follow our inner urges, through the exclusion of external validation, we will find ourselves in new beginnings over and over again forcing us to listen internally.

KEN – relates to *Mountain*. It holds the qualities of stillness, resting, meditating and tranquility. It is immobile and represents beginnings and endings. Its characteristic animal is the *Dog* representing loyalty, faithfulness and guardianship. The period begins approximately February first. Its personality is *Still* and its family position is the *Youngest Son*. In Feng Shui the aspect of life is *Wisdom*.

Once an endeavor has been initiated, guidelines for action and behavior need to be established to build a structure that will carry the energy through the cycle. What has been heard, internally, must now be envisioned to enable a template for creation. The only way to focus on this is to "go inside" and turn off all external input that might tarnish or disturb the pureness of creativity. Simplicity is the key. Simplicity can be found in silence. Since the *Youngest Son* has no external rules or guidelines that he feels he has to follow, he can be the clearest in the way he creates *unless* he is reactive and rebels against the existing structure. By reacting he polarizes himself and becomes as limited as the rules he rebels against. If reactive, he then *needs* the silence to hear the internal voice. In the I Ching the Hexagram portrayed is symbol 52, mountain over mountain, which is called "Keeping Still." To him the world is silent except for what *he* sets in motion. He is "spoiled" by his family and "self centered" to an extreme. The *Youngest Son* is, usually, hyper, active and in need of learning silence. However, he has the advantage of being totally absorbed by his own feelings and, hence, totally focused. He can be the epitome of the *Mountain*. His internal sense of self is eminently stubborn and strongly rooted in his feelings for the vision which creates his intentions. Now the Dog, the symbol of fidelity, comes into play. His fidelity is to the vision sensed in the internal silence and the values, methods and structure that lead him to its manifestation.

So we can now say that once the vision has been understood, or at least conceptualized, we must arrange our lives in a way that reflects that path and utilizes the values that will lead to its formation. Meditation or *Keeping Still,* internally, will give us the best avenue to this. The task is to discriminate between instinct, which is reactive to the emotional triggers of rebelliousness, and intuition which comes without the emotional restrictions.

CHEN – relates to *Thunder*. It portrays an arousing, movement, activity, shock, voracious growth, and swiftness. Its characteristic animal is the *Dragon* representing soaring and stormy skies. It should be pointed out here that the western dragon is very different from the oriental dragon. For the west the dragon represents terror, destruction and fear. For the east it represents power, virility and fortune. The period of the year begins on the spring equinox. Its personality is *Arousing* and its family position is the *Eldest Son*. In Feng Shui the aspect of life is *Family*.

The idea has been conceived and the format for the creation has been decided and committed to. Now that the energy is no longer being used for the formation of a plan toward the goal, it is now free to be used in actually manifesting the creation. Everything is now channeled into physical growth. The *Dragon* within is *Aroused* and a tremendous force is applied to this creation. This force is the life energy contained within the *Dragon* in its clearest and most potent form. The results of its application are shocking in its intensity and swiftness. The Chinese Hexagram that results from the pairing of thunder over thunder is symbol #51 called "The Arousing" or "Shocking" as if a clap of thunder were to startle us. It's like a huge army has been directed with a single objective and with complete single mindedness. With a very clear set of values and expectations to be fulfilled, similar to the expectations a father has of his *Eldest Son*, the creation has taken form almost as if over night. The plan has been fulfilled with a passion and intensity that could have only been inspired by knowing exactly what needs to be done. The *Eldest Son* follows the format of the only pattern known…tradition. Having tradition has made it easy to know what to do but the results are wholly generic and expected. It is a rough hewn creation. These older historical structures are the only formats available for emulation. As such, their application may be outdated for the needs of the creation's refinement. Nevertheless, the tidal wave has passed and gentler currents are approaching.

Now that we have conceptualized our vision and set the rules and values down for its creation in Ken, we may now put our full force into the tangible manifestation of it in Chen. We can produce the foundation and structure needed through the combination and integration of our abilities, resources and intentions. This comes by faithfully rendering its building according to our visionary blueprint.

SUN – relates to *Wind*. It exhibits gentle efforts, small efforts and penetrating work. Its characteristic animal is the *Rooster* representing piercing the stillness and a watchman. The period of the year begins approximately on May Day. Its personality is *Gentle* and the family position is the *Eldest Daughter*. In Feng Shui the aspect of life is *Self Empowerment & Wealth*.

The voracious growth of the last part of the cycle begins to slow in speed and intensity. The creation has taken shape. However, this fulfillment has been very rudimentary and simply defined. It needs to be "colored" or "personalized" with the characteristic qualities of the creator. This is where we see an individuation of the creation that distinguishes it from other creations. Picture a home that has just been built and is in need of paint, carpets and furnishings to accommodate and reflect the tastes of a specific inhabitant. The home will, now, take on a personality of its own. It will have its own flair. The I Ching shows this as wind over wind being symbol #57 relating to "Gentle Penetration" and showing the slow but perpetual effect of a gentle wind on the landscape making individualistic changes over a long period of time while adding character and specificity of function. In a sense, the artist has blocked the canvas, laid down the basic colors, the background and outlined the image of the vision to be produced. Now it's time for him to give his creation defining features to show character and to evoke a style that is recognizable to others as his alone. Following his inner vision reflects the gentleness and the inner sensitivity of the *Eldest Daughter* and the manifestation of the creation expresses the boldness and distinguishing characteristics of the self promoting *Rooster*. This might be from where we derive the expression "full of hot air" as applied to an egotistic *Rooster*.

Now that we have conceptualized, planned and constructed our creation we can now put the finishing touches on our project that best say, "This is who I am." This will become our personal expression and individual signature for this cycle. Its refined qualities will be what distinguish us from others who work on the same creation. It has required us to listen carefully to the small voice within so that the qualities of its completion will match the original intuitive conceptualization at the beginning of the cycle as closely as possible.

Upon our creation's arrival at its peak of expression the focus of attention must, now, shift away from the process of *projecting and building*. The next four parts must now switch to emphasizing *listening* and *receiving* feedback from the universe as to how our creation has contributed to or detracted from the natural flow of nature. Since we in the west are, essentially, pragmatic "do" people we have, thus far, had very few problems handling the first four parts. Now there comes a crisis in our awareness. Are we able to let go and let nature speak to us without attempting to adjust its message to suit our expectations and continuing in our obsession by improving it with more "doing?" Can we be satisfied with the way the universe views us? Can we now receive?

LI – relates to *Fire*. It provides illumination, clarity, drying, intelligence, dependence and attachment. Its characteristic animal is the *Pheasant* representing brightness and exposure. The period begins on the summer solstice. Its personality is *Clinging* and its family position is the *Middle Daughter*. In Feng Shui the aspect of life is *Fame*.

At this point our creation has been manifested as well as it could possibly have been. The resources that were available to apply to this creation have begun to recede and any possibility of "improving" on its quality has moved past the opportunity for doing so. It has reached the "point of no return." This is where the artist steps back and assesses his own work. He must now, also, let go and allow the universe to react to its beauty and usefulness as it will. It is now up to us to switch our focus from "giving" to "receiving." The *Pheasant* has spread its tail in its fullest majesty. All is seen and all is known by the brilliance of the *Fire* and the noontime sun. As in nature our creation has arrived at the point of its most visible splendor or most obvious horror. It is what it is and we must accept it as such. This is the point in the cycle that westerners have the most difficulty transitioning through. We are such a pragmatic "do" culture that we cannot bear to let something stand in its own nakedness. We feel we must perpetually improve on it or explain its perceived and assumed deficiencies. In essence, we feel that we must maintain control of its existence at all costs. We find that we are persistent in *Clinging* to it as a reflection of our identity as shown by Hexagram #30. This is the same as a mother who must finally let her child walk or fall on his own. We have given life to something and now it is time for it to find its place in the world. It will now become categorized and judged by others and acquire a reputation. It enters the realm of *Fame* and is noticed by the world. In this the *Middle Daughter*, who receives the least amount of attention from her family (the world), withdraws from the limelight and through her obvious withdrawal receives the notice and attention she dreads.

We have now reached the point where our creation must now become part of the world. We must let it go. We must look at its value and usefulness in the brightest of light. We must now allow others to react to us as they feel. We must now "objectively" assess its effect on the world. In this we must risk being judged by others. We must now acknowledge our pride in our creation. Comparison is our worst enemy. We must now integrate our creation into the world and let it be absorbed.

K'UN – relates to *Earth*. Its qualities are yielding, receptive, responsive, devoted and submissive. Its characteristic animal is the *Cow* representing gentleness. The period begins approximately August first. Its personality is *Receptive* and its family position is the *Mother*. In Feng Shui the aspect of life is *Relationships*.

The hardest point in the cycle, for the western mind, has been confronted and hopefully handled. We now turn our sights to outside of our personal perceptions. Not only are we looking for feedback about our creation but we are seeking an understanding of how it will be used by others and why. We are heightening our *Receptive* qualities as illustrated in Hexagram #2. We are listening with a sense for what is needed by others to integrate our creation into the wholeness of things. This "first harvest" is the first time we are aware of what the world needs or desires from us in order to deal with what we offer. It's the first time we are listening to determine what to give so the world will run more smoothly and, in a sense, seeking how to nurture the world. In this light we see the characteristics of the *Cow*; the most nurturing of all mammals. We also find, as a "byproduct," that listening requires a poise of gentleness. This is the first experience of a conscious service and stewardship in this cycle. The qualities of gentleness, nurturance, submissiveness, devotion & "unconditional" sensitivity are qualities exhibited by a *Mother*. Now that we have two personal perceptions interchanging energy and "commerce," we see the beginnings of a reciprocal *Relationship*; a give and take, a melding of energies.

We now understand how and if our creation is needed by the world and what must be done to integrate it as such. To complete this requires attentiveness, humility and a genuine state of receptivity. If many wish what we have to provide, we are at risk of becoming egotistical about our "offerings." This is no reflection on our value as a human since when what we have to offer is finished so, too, is our "popularity." We must remember that we are no better and no worse than any other.

TUI – relates to the *Lake*. It portrays a joy, openness, pleasure, satisfaction and all excess. Its characteristic animal is the *Sheep* representing the concubine. The period begins on the fall equinox. Its personality is *Joyous* and its family position is the *Youngest Daughter*. In Feng Shui the aspect of life is *Creativity & Children*.

We begin to observe the integration of our creation into the world. It has been assessed for "usefulness" and ease of use. As it peaks in applicability, the increasing demand for it begins to wane. Instinctively we look for ways to keep it at its crest of popularity. To do this we start to adjust to the needs and demands of those using it. We, in essence, become the *Sheep*, much like a concubine, expecting our action to be compensated for by its continued support and use. We and our creation become like a *Lake* and adapt its shape to fit the current container or form of need. We, gradually, give up parts of our prior expectations and begin to accept that it has reached its peak in value. We give up focusing on our prior requirements and direct our resources to the needs of our *Children* and the world to which we have given our creation and we do this with pleasure and satisfaction. In the same way, as the required responsibilities of the *Youngest Daughter* are minimized by the establishment of the family structure before she arrived, we recognize that the needs and responsibilities for maintaining our creation are past the time of being necessary. Having little responsibility left leaves us feeling *Joyous* as portrayed by the hexagram #58. This enables us to approach life with innocence and openness.

Our creation has been integrated into the world and no longer requires our stewardship. We must accept its passage into antiquity with grace and gratitude. We give up the final threads of whatever control and identity we had that connected us to it. It now belongs to the world and it will morph into a state that is beyond our vision. We are free to look ahead toward a new vision and creation.

CH'IEN – relates to *Heaven*. It exhibits firmness, creativity, strength, force and power. Its characteristic animal is the *Horse* representing swiftness and tirelessness. The period begins on approximately Halloween. Its personality is *Creative* and its family position is the *Father*. In Feng Shui the aspect of life is *Helpful People*.

We have "processed" our creation through the world. We must now focus on a new cycle. This involves preparation and foresight. The first task that must be undertaken before we can formulate a new project is to clear any parts of the prior one that might create a block or obstruction. Otherwise the remnants of the last project may present themselves as barriers to the new creative process. This may be likened to having a ball and chain attached to our leg as we begin a new journey. If the past journey was to remain grounded during a windstorm, then the ball and chain were applicable then and considered an asset at the time. However, if the new project requires the ability to move with agility, they would then become a tremendous liability. Our new focus is to remove the remnants of the old structures. This requires that we muster up the energy to clear ourselves, also. In one way *Helpful People* provide this kind of energy and assistance to us for removing the obstacles to accomplishing our objectives. In a symbolic way, the *Horse* may be considered similar kind of energy with the necessary strength to aid us in clearing and tilling the earth by breaking the topsoil tension in order soften the soil and provide a fertile growing medium for the new seed. In any event, the process involves redistributing the remaining resources we accumulated for our past project back into the world to be used elsewhere. This leaves us free and clear with unfettered energy and tremendous uncommitted power to apply to the new creation. The *Father* represents the spirit of a clear, active and *Creative* energy as symbolized by Hexagram #1.

Our objective is the acquisition of the wisdom and power of the empty cup. To do this we must purge ourselves of anything that may color our ability to assess. Fasting, meditation and vision quests are a few examples of how this energy would show itself. This allows a clear path for visions of the future.

As with any other set of cycles, this one will repeat end over end. It could divide the cycle of the day, a year, lifetime or even a millennium. In any even, the parts will divide fairly evenly as symbolized by the types of changing perspectives and events within the cycle. Let's move now to the last model I will use; the Lunar Phases.

LUNAR PHASES:
THE BLUEPRINT FOR THE PHYSICAL UNIVERSE

Since the phases of the moon have such a dramatic effect on the tides of the earth, which is more than half water, it follows reason that they should also have at least as much of an effect on our physical bodies which are more than seventy percent water. If we also accept the premise that our emotions are highly comparable to the movement of water we can begin to see how we are subject to the same, seemingly subtle yet tangible, changes in force and energy around us. Since we are within the energy sphere of the earth we must also feel and go through what she does. Essentially, we act like "little Earths." As humans, we also go through seasons. Two things must be pointed out here. First, have you ever noticed that people and dogs that have been with each other over a long period of time start to look and act like each other? And people who have been married a long time also look and feel like each other? So, living beings that share the same space, eventually, exhibit the same characteristics. Wouldn't it follow that they would also share the same moods or emotions? In metaphysical law this is called, "The law of induction or entrainment." The second metaphysical law states, "As above so below." What this means is that whatever exists within the sphere of the other follows the same laws. Essentially, if we look at nature on a larger scale (cosmic) or on a smaller scale (cellular) they will follow the same pattern and laws. As an example, consider the curious comparison between the atom, its electrons and the orbits that they inhabit and our solar system, the Sun and the orbits that the planets inhabit. The movement and pattern is the same just slower since it's on a larger scale. On a cellular level we can see the pattern of mitosis and on the planetary scale, the march of the seasons. Consequently, they also follow the same patterns. The phases of the Moon are a visible, tangible example of this pattern that everything in the universe follows. You may call this inductive or deductive reasoning depending on which approach you take. You may, also, disagree by saying that there is no "tangible" proof that this is so but, nevertheless, you can't help observe that there is a fascinating similarity between these patterns on all levels in the universe. This eight fold system will serve to set the template for the rest of this book. With this understanding firmly in place, let's examine the eight phases of the Moon.

EMERGENCE - New Moon - the keyword for this phase is the unknown. This is the beginning of a totally new experience and will be entirely subjective. The impulse to new action comes *only* from within. It is powered by impulse, emotion and intuition. Any action we take must come from our inner guidance or instinct. As the seed is totally encased in darkness of earth with no perception of what surrounds it, so are we as we conceive a new idea or project. To sense or "see" this vision we must be internally focused with no disturbance from the external world. There are no external signposts to guide us in this uncharted territory. In a personal sense we may feel more alone during this cycle than any other, yet, it includes more freedom than of any of the other phases as it is the most unmanifest as of yet. The requirement here is of concentration, focus and a sense of withdrawing within to "allow" the vision to penetrate our awareness fully. It requires a purity of innocence that can be found in the tarot deck as represented by the Fool.

ASSERTION - Crescent Moon – the keywords for this phase are planning, commitment and value. It is here that we set up a framework that will perpetuate the values and format needed to transform our new impulse into a reality. Creating an organized plan will create a standard to help us stay focused and to overcome any obstacles to our new vision.

This phase requires that we have faith in our ability to handle whatever may come as a result of pursuing our vision. As we assert ourselves we will appear challenging to any other "system" that is accepted and in play with others. This is also the time that we are the most vulnerable to subversion and selling out to others in order to feel a sense of belonging and being accepted. If we are to succeed we must follow our personal values and stand our ground. The requirement here is one of commitment and meditation.

ACTION - 1st Quarter Moon – the keywords here are raw manifestation and growth. We may not have all the details but instinctively we know what must be done to flesh out the framework needed for our vision. This is the first physical representation of our vision and is the most physically forceful of all the phases. Tremendous energy feeds a laser focused drive almost to the point of ruthlessness. Anything standing in the way risks obliteration. There is almost a warrior mentality that focuses on purging the old and forging the new in its most basic form with lightning action. The requirement here is of accelerated physical growth, focus and vigorous exercise.

EXPRESSION - Gibbous Moon – the keywords here are refinement and personal signature. This is where the manifested vision takes on detailed characteristics specific to its author so there are no mistakes as to whose vision it is. In this way the vision finds it's most individual expression. This is the last opportunity to "improve" upon it. It is here that its "fate" is sealed. This phase corresponds to the artist within all of us. It also colors and classifies our expression in the eyes of our social structure and leads toward being labeled and associated with specific group characteristics. This builds family. Taken to an extreme an exaggeration of this expression could lead to an egotistical unorthodoxy. The requirement here is of developing breath control and overcoming instincts.

FULFILLMENT - Full Moon – the keywords here are visible and revealed. The Moon in this position is literally opposite the Sun. The opposition, in astrological terms, is symbolic of relationships. As with an honest relationship everything is clear, visible and obvious. What was intuited is now confirmed. Having completed our vision we now face a crisis in perspective. It is much like a college student who finally graduates. He must now cease applying energy to his completed four year goal and the familiar "nest" it supplied and apply his energy and what he has learned to the "outside" world. It is the same with our vision. We must disengage from our creative momentum and let our creation join the world and accept the world's judgment of it. It is past the time for the availability to make any more improvements. This will, most likely, bring a sense of loss, emptiness and disorientation since our tendency is to cling to our creation as it has defined our identity in creative terms for the term of its building. The requirement here is for introspection, acceptance and a deep letting go.

SYNTHESIS - Disseminating Moon – The keywords here are humility, adaptation and usefulness. Not everyone is going to be able to use or appreciate our creation. So, what can we do to make it more accessible, enjoyable and useful to others? The more homogeneous we make it, the less character it will retain. But is that really important? At this point, to integrate our creation into the flow of our natural social structure would give the best complement as to its usefulness. This action would also connect with the nurturing part of our natures. It requires us to listen and accept the feedback of what is needed. This is the test of our receptivity since our response will be the gauge by which we are assessed as to how well we allow our project's synthesizing back into the social milieu. The requirement here is of blending, education and, most emphatically, the elimination of egotistical pride as related to our project.

REORIENTATION - 3rd Quarter Moon – The keywords here are adjustment, revamping and tailoring. We are aware of the parts of our social group that our creation fits well with but we are, also, painfully aware of where it does not. We must be careful to allow the needed new focus, gauged toward a new and different future, to take precedence over our, now past, creation. We must not insist that its character remain in tact as a reflection of our ego even if it has *not* outlived its usefulness. This is a deeper and more compassionate form of letting go. We cannot insist on preservation for posterity. There is a gearing up for the future where our sacrifices will pave the way. We know, instinctively, of the new cycle that is coming and must address it in a clean and clear manner. Here we may inspire others to transcend the limitations of the dying present cycle. The requirement here is reorganizing and cooperation.

RELEASE - Balsamic Moon – The keywords here are foresight, preparation and purgation. Of all the phases this is the most intangibly received and the most tangibly directed. It is a total anticipation of the new cycle by clearing all obstacles to its intuited structure. There is a sense of "destiny" almost as if one were led by a "higher power." It feels as if we are the vehicle through which something higher is taking place. We accept the passing of relationships, circumstances and security with the confidence that something of more import and usefulness will take their place. There is a sense of never ending preparing. There is an unseen vision waiting to be born in an aspect of transition. The requirement is of purification, preparation and allowing the inner self to direct us.

With the Moon phases, the eight Bagua of the I Ching and the pagan holidays and seasons we have three formats to frame our understanding of how life moves through the natural cycle. In the *Part II* I have integrated them phase by phase to make it easier to concentrate on each phase individually. Joe's apartment is a tangible example of how these phases apply to a common life experience.

JOE'S NEW APARTMENT
A PRACTICAL EXAMPLE

Joe has been living in his apartment for quite some time. He has been very comfortable but has been finding that lately he needs a change of venue to stimulate his creativity. One night it was if a light bulb went off in his head. Out of the blue the possibility of moving *emerged* from somewhere deep inside of him. It kind of tickled him to realize that this was such an obvious solution to shaking up his life and environment with new energy. It wasn't until he was just sitting quietly that it just "bubbled" up from inside of him. He continued to sit quietly and let images and possibilities surface. A dog was barking somewhere because the neighbors were having an argument but Joe kept his concentration on that quiet spot within. The images came quickly and easily but as quickly as they came were as quickly as they changed. He watched it like a movie; not trying to rationalize or categorize anything but just paying attention. After a while he had accumulated a whole array of images for possible floor plans. As the images tapered off he began to sift through what he had received. He began to lay out a plan. He made a list of requirements to give to his real estate agent and he drafted a letter to his landlord expressing his intentions. He had to work through a few bugs with his landlord since the lease wasn't straight forward but he stuck to his guns and *asserted* himself about what he wanted and the landlord eventually agreed.

After a short time his real estate agent found a couple of apartments that fit his specifications so he took *action* by surveying the apartments, contracting for one of them, finalizing his agreement with his new land lord and having a moving company move his furniture while he boxed up and moved all his personal belongings. The whole event took three days in a whirlwind of activity. When he was done he had to actively slow himself down from the momentum. As the intensity waned he began to unpack. After the basics were distributed to their appropriately useful locations he positioned all his personal items throughout his apartment to create a sense of comfort and familiarity. He also painted and bought some new furnishings to make his apartment an *expression* of his unique nature and character. With his environment arranged and filled with his worldly possessions there was nothing left for him to do. He felt *fulfilled* that his new abode was an effective expression of his true personal nature. It was now time to invite his friends and work associates over to work and be entertained and for him to hear their opinions about his new home. He prepared, adjusted and straightened his apartment to the last possible moment before they arrived. There was no more opportunity to improve. The world was upon him. Some liked it. Some didn't and they each had different reasons. Joe was getting feedback on his creative endeavor.

Joe has been working for a company where he works in groups with others. Many times they congregate at his home to conduct company business. Generally, he has four or five workers at one time. His apartment worked well for quite a few months as he had planned a good arrangement with plenty of space. But as his business grew so did the number of workers he needed to work with. This made it necessary to rearrange the apartment and bring furniture together from other rooms to accommodate the increased number of people. He *synthesized* the expanded needs of his company with the current usefulness of his apartment by making many small adjustments. As the month pressed on the co-workers changed over and Joe came to find that a larger number of them came from a farther distance than the previous ones. To make things easier he decided it would be best to meet at another worker's home closer to the majority of their homes. This made it easier for them but more time consuming for Joe in travel time. He also had to *reorient* his schedule to account for this extra time needed to travel to the new location. His "new" apartment was no longer serving as well as it had in the previous months. Since his job was extremely rewarding and important he began to think that another move would make things easier for everyone including himself. It would also relieve other workers of having to host his meetings. After a while he decided that the move would be in everyone's best interest. This would allow him to get a larger apartment at a better location to host the larger number of workers. He *released* the expectations he had had for his comfy apartment and resigned himself to finding a new environment to accommodate the newly developed needs. He would begin a new cycle by moving to a new location, meeting a new group of neighbors and find new places to frequent for his shopping and enjoyment needs.

URANUS:
THE LIFE CLOCK & THE "BIG" PICTURE

Having defined the structure of a cycle from three different perspectives and given a tangible example we now move on to a new template to work with. This new template will now provide a clock to affix to our cycle. This will allow us to define times for sensitive periods and likely events.

Each planet in our solar system revolves around the Sun but each takes a different amount of time to do so. After the Moon, the planet most commonly used for timing is Saturn. But at this juncture I would like to digress from the usual progression of astrological tradition and focus on our least traditional planet Uranus. I call him our Life Clock. His eighty four year cycle roughly follows the current human life expectancy. Three Saturn cycles of twenty eight years each fit within the Uranus cycle which I will cover later. Uranus' eighty four years divides into eight ten and one half year phases. The points of change are at ten and a half, twenty one, thirty one and a half, forty two, fifty two and a half, sixty three, and seventy three and a half. Age eighty four begins a new cycle again.

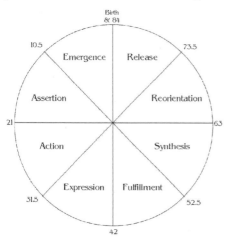

Uranus' cycle follows our social progression of expected life changes. This is true regardless whether a person is conscious of them or not. Since we are very materialistic beings we live and accept the cycle of Saturn more easily than we can accept or even fathom the dynamics of Uranus. Traditionally, Uranus has been considered the planet of unconventionality and the unexpected. But, since he is such an arch "enemy" of Saturn's predictable and expected plodding through our lives, occurrences that coincide with his transits, almost always, come as a surprise. The outer, or trans Saturnian planets, have always been difficult, at best, for us to deal with since they so rarely follow our materialistic projections like Saturn and the planets within his orbit do. Their effects can be seen but only in a longer range of focus and deeper perspective of connectedness. With this understanding that Uranus operates from a, seemingly, less obvious place than those *within* his orbit, let's continue to examine the Life Clock phases that he symbolizes.

EMERGENCE: Our birth is, probably, the singular most important "sudden occurrence" event that Uranus can portray other than our death. As we are born we are totally unaware of life and what is expected of us...from a physical world perspective. Uranus is a planet that is representative of energy and its unobservable causes. But remember that as a new born baby we still exist in that spirit energy world until we get grounded in the accepted world of materialism. We, for some time, will still see the energies and spirits on the "other side" and we will, slowly, become desensitized to them as we are subjected to the relentless, forced acceptance of the physical world as being all that is important in life on Earth. Is it any wonder that we may feel lost and need to be led as there are no sign posts showing how to function in this foreign world we have newly arrived in? We must totally rely on the combination of our inner knowing and the tutorage of a guide in the physical world (usually our parents) until we can frame our patterns for coping. In this respect we can see how Uranus is considered to be the best representative of innovativeness and creativity in the conventional astrological world. As we come into this life with a relatively blank slate it's, also, easy to see how our formative patterns can become so easily and deeply ingrained since nothing has filled the space yet. We are eager, open and unblocked. This is truly the most, originally, creative time.

ASSERTION: At ten and a half we encounter one of our most physical and assertive awakenings; puberty. The assertive influence of this phase becomes poignantly apparent as our roll in this world becomes solidly defined as to what is expected of us. Granted, with the advent of open homosexuality and unisex issues it may not be as socially well defined as one would wish but as for nature and our connection to it there remains no doubt as to what is expected of us; continuity of our species. It is also here that our values, limitations and prospective growth take on their most solid form. Our diets, hormones, training and part of the world we live in all have a profound affect on how we define our participation in life. All these factors will contribute to how we assert our position in our new world. In nature this should be where we take on our roll in the natural evolution of our species but our social structure has demanded that we remain in this period called adolescence until we are assessed as being indoctrinated enough in the ways of society's physical world so we will participate in it as it *is* rather than adjust it back to a way that is in harmony with nature. (This phase coincides with Saturn's first *Expression* phase).

ACTION: Up to this point we have been seen and not heard...or at least, not listened to. At twenty one we are now accepted by our culture as being trained, matured and "qualified" enough to participate in the world as a contributing entity. We are now "legal." This phase is the first quarter which activates the most physical of participation. This is, generally, the time that those of us who have gone to college, graduate. It is the age that we can vote, drink, own things and take advantage of all that our indoctrination has been preparing us for. It is now that our careers will take off, or at least, are supposed to. We are now fully expected to carry our share of the load of supporting ourselves *and* expected to, and usually do, produce offspring that will repeat the pattern. Healthy or not, this is the time of the most intense physical, mental and emotional change. (This phase coincides with Saturn's first *Reorientation* phase).

EXPRESSION: By thirty one and a half most of us have chosen and entered a career, gotten married, had a child or two and are on our way to fulfilling the "American Dream" or the ideal life of whatever culture we belong to. Some of us are very satisfied to belong to the status quo living "snug as a bug" in a secure, predetermined structure. Others of us are not satisfied with that alone. We begin to feel there must be something more than just paying the bills, building a pension and looking good to the neighbors. We become a bit disillusioned as to performing the way our social "clan" has dictated and are asking ourselves how are we different? How are we unique, or not, from everyone else who's following the same path? We begin to look for ways to put our personal stamp on our career. We want to make it a reflection of our perceived uniqueness. We look for ways to do things that will get notice from those of our group while some of us do it in a more conservative way and others of us express it in a more unorthodox way. We look at our children and decide we want something better for them. We want them to be different and have some of the options we didn't have and want to prevent them from making some of the same "mistakes" that we believe we've made. At this time we become much more susceptible to the judgment of our "clan" and the surrounding social groups as we express our individuality. (This phase coincides with Saturn's second *Assertion* phase).

FULFILLMENT: At forty two there comes a crisis. This is what most people, laughingly, refer to as a mid-life crisis. This is no laughing matter. (This is not only when Uranus opposes itself but transiting Saturn and the progressed Moon makes their second opposition to themselves at *Fulfillment*) and Neptune makes its first square to itself at *Action*). Our life is at the point of no return…half way. For the first forty two years we have worked toward creating what we thought we wanted with the values and mindset we've adopted as our own. Since this is the time of "full moon," it is a time where all becomes apparent; how we fit into the world, how we don't, our future prospects based on current attitudes and, finally, facing ourselves in this light. At this age most of our kids are at their *Action* phase and are out of the house or close to being so. As they move into their independent lives (hopefully) we have less and less focus on them and more on ourselves, our mates and what that life has amounted to, thus far, in our judgment and that of our peers and those we consider our elders and/or "superiors." If we like what we have created we continue with our plan and proceed into the future with confidence. If we don't, we either participate in activities that distract us from looking at ourselves or we assess our situation and decide what plans must be put into place to make our lives more to our liking and expectations. In distracting ourselves men may absorb themselves in toys, women plunge into shopping and both my find younger relationships that they can feel more in control of and revisit earlier patterns they participated in before their newly realized awareness. The assessment of accomplishment, or not, comes with the opposition. The Neptune square (*Action* phase) brings the inner, intangible part of life much more into focus. We begin to look for more than just the survival, support and tangible aspects of life and begin to listen to our feelings about our participation in life. We ask ourselves if it's in line with what *we* feel is important while asking *what* is important. We will be faced with the question of what to let go of after our assessment. As it is with the Moon's *Fulfillment* phase, we, of the western world, are still ill equipped to be able to let go easily. It is at this time that any long term efforts that go against our natural inclination toward health start to grow and show themselves as disease. Ignored, they still grow beneath our awareness. Feared they accelerate. This could be poor life style relative to career or social activities, the long term effects of the environments we subject ourselves to and, lastly, ignoring bodily signals that tell us of its need for attention or change in order to maintain a healthy state. This is truly a time for crucial assessment as this will dictate how the whole "reaping" phase of life proceeds.

SYNTHESIS: At fifty two and a half we generally feel accepting of what we have accomplished and how we have adjusted its presentation to the world. At this age we take on the mentoring and training of others in the work that we have done in anticipation of leaving the work in capable hands when we retire. It is here that we take our knowledge of life and people and pass it on to others. Since this information falls into the hands and minds of a new generation it will morph into something we are not familiar with. We must be nurturing but not possessive. We must accept that they may see new potential for its use that we were formerly unaware of. Life and our creations will evolve whether we want them to or not. We must be receptive to what is needed by others if they are to use what it is we offer. This is a test of our acquired humility and diminished ego. If we attempt to maintain control or demand that our creation be used in a way that we feel the most secure, we will meet with tremendous resistance and, occasionally, become ostracized from precisely the group we want to maintain our interest in. Worse yet, our creation may be dropped for someone who is easier to deal with and more amenable toward contemporary applications. If, in examining ourselves, we find our status lacking in the image that we want to project to our public, we will be totally unable to be receptive to the needs of others except for the confirmation of the image we need or want to project. This whole phase is about yielding control to the younger generation so they can use and adapt our creation to everyone's best advantage.

REORIENTATION: We are now at sixty three years old. This is generally retirement age where we are expected to abdicate any controlling interest we have in the prevailing career arena and move to the "sidelines" and allow the new blood to take our creation to new heights. We are expected to have made our nest egg and have it provide what we need. We are also expected to invest financially and emotionally in the success of those who follow us. At this point we are, literally, beginning to live our life in a completely different fashion; taking time for personal desires and needs which have not been afforded the time or opportunity in the past as we were developing our career. If we have followed the American dream everything is assumed to be in place to live our life separated from our career and in a relaxed fashion. If we have not been living the American dream, as many have not, we have to change gears and continue to participate in the working world. Many will have to maintain additional employment to survive as disappearing and failing pension plans and social security are insufficient to keep pace with the rising cost of living. We must become much more resourceful in order to keep a place in the world. As more commodities are produced outside the country it becomes necessary to work more within the "service" world as they are the only remaining options. Some are resourceful enough to commence home businesses. The *Reorientation* required has been becoming more of a challenge since the traditional patterns of retirement have lost their presence while a more uncertain and unknowable future takes its place.

RELEASE: At seventy three and a half we've played enough golf and shuffle board to choke a horse. Since we've had a lot more time to participate in the world in a much more relaxed and detached fashion (forced or voluntary) we have become much more aware of our mortality and we begin to think about where our possessions and resources will go to after we are gone. We are very concerned about how and where we *Release* what we have been attached to. This phase and the two proceeding are harvest phases. However, the material part of the harvest is not so much for the person going through the phases as it is for the people they affect and leave their creations to. The key to the harvest phases, for the person going through them, is the recognition of potential freedom and power as the need for control is gradually released. As more attention and attempted control is released from past applications, more energy is available for health, awareness and any new applications. This being recognized, our candidates begin to actively divest themselves of all worldly connections in order to prepare and build energy and focus for the new direction implied by the ending of this cycle and the beginning of the next. This culminates at, approximately, eighty four years of age or death. Consider the *healthy* adults (physically *and* mentally) that you have witnessed achieving the age of eighty four. They usually become playful, willful, adventurous children, either by what appears to be "mental aberration" or conscious, aware choice.

As the preceding cycles give ages of transition please be aware that these ages may vary even up to five years either direction of the prospective timing for a change. Uranus' orbit is not an exact distance from the Sun at all points so the cycle may seem to slow down in some signs and speed up in others. This unevenness is the most apparent in Pluto's orbit since it is more exaggerated by being an elliptical orbit. Uranus has, not only, a slightly elliptical orbit but also, in its transits, as with the other planets, goes into retrograde, to station and to direct motion. This causes further irregularities in the timing of our transitioning phases and may contact a change point more than once in a life due to this zigzagging effect. Additionally, much like aspects and their orbs, the *approach* to the change point cusp, or applying aspect, is more potent than after it has passed.

01 Ar	16 Ta	01 Can	16 Le	01 Li	16 Sc	01 Cap	16 Aq
02 Ar	17 Ta	02 Can	17 Le	02 Li	17 Sc	02 Cap	17 Aq
03 Ar	18 Ta	03 Can	18 Le	03 Li	18 Sc	03 Cap	18 Aq
04 Ar	19 Ta	04 Can	19 Le	04 Li	19 Sc	04 Cap	19 Aq
05 Ar	20 Ta	05 Can	20 Le	05 Li	20 Sc	05 Cap	20 Aq
06 Ar	21 Ta	06 Can	21 Le	06 Li	21 Sc	06 Cap	21 Aq
07 Ar	22 Ta	07 Can	22 Le	07 Li	22 Sc	07 Cap	22 Aq
08 Ar	23 Ta	08 Can	23 Le	08 Li	23 Sc	08 Cap	23 Aq

To make it easier to determine at what might be looked at as the exact ages and where the change points occur, I've constructed a table. There is the 45 Degree Table on page 110 and 111 of this book. Take a quick look, now, and come back to this point. The preceding is a portion of this table.

We will use this table to find the eight zodiacal points and dates at which Uranus will change phase. As an example, let's start with a natal position for transiting Saturn of five degrees of Cancer. Please look to the abbreviated chart and find this point. This will be the *Emergence* phase. To find the *Assertion* phase just look to the right to twenty degrees of Leo. Each move to the right is forty five degrees equaling one phase. Follow through phase by phase until you have all the points. When you move on from twenty degrees of Aquarius simply wrap around on the other side of the chart with five degrees of Aries for the *Reorientation* phase and continue until you have all the phases. Your completed chart should look like the one above. With these points determined we can now look up the dates for each time Uranus contacts these points. This will give us the personal calendar of change points for the client with Uranus at five degrees of Cancer.

I still cannot emphasize enough that the changes that come with each new phase happen in a very gradual process. The inner planets will serve as the "triggers" for circumstances that will start to make these changes apparent in the tangible world. The Uranus cycle will serve as a stage or backdrop coloring and flavoring the corresponding actions of the planets they hold.

The first two "heavies" I want to focus on are transiting Saturn and the progressing moon. These two planets and their movement serve as the foundation and structure for our worldly actions and circumstances. You will also notice that I will redundantly refer to them as "transiting" and "progressing." This is not by accident. This labeling may feel annoying after a time but please realize that I am attempting to devalue static interpretation and instill an awareness of the dynamic quality inherent in their continuous movement.

TRANSITING SATURN:
THE TANGIBLE CLOCK

Saturn is the planet that symbolizes material issues. Roughly, he follows three twenty eight year cycles within the Uranian eighty four year cycle that is currently accepted as the approximate current life expectancy for humans. The first twenty eight years we become aware, through the world's reflection, of who we are and what we have to work with within the tangible world. The second twenty eight years, from twenty eight to fifty six, we become productive with what we have learned. The last twenty eight years, from fifty six to eighty four, we become a healer, teacher and guidance counselor with what we have learned and, hopefully, mastered.

The PROGRESSING MOON:
THE INTERNAL PERCEIVER

The progressing moon reflects our changing perspective of how we feel about ourselves and the world. She, also, follows three, approximately, twenty eight year cycles within the Uranian cycle. The first twenty eight years we develop our opinions and beliefs about how we fit, or not, in the external world. The second twenty eight years we follow through on and evolve the validity of those judgments. The last twenty eight years we have the opportunity to see how those assessments created a folding (blocking) or unfolding (promoting) of circumstances leading toward or away from wisdom.

NUMEROLOGY and the SUB-CYCLES
WHY SHOULD ASTROLOGY HAVE ALL THE FUN?

Up until this point we have seen how three different disciplines co-respond to each other through the patterning of cycles except from different perspectives. Since all of these delineations show their effectiveness through the mathematical division of the natural cycle it seems only fair to show the connection to numerology. However, this connection is not quite as exacting as the prior disciplines in this way. Modern numerology operates a on a cycle of nine. This, obviously, does not fit into the working scheme of things. Yet, if we look back at the Chaldeans and the ancient system of numbers, they worked with a cycle of eight. They believed that the number nine was a number of finality and that could only be attributed to God. This may make sense if you look at the fact that, in the contemporary use of numerology, any number that you add to nine remains the same. As an example, if you add four to nine the total is thirteen. Following numerological form you would continue adding until you arrived at one digit. Hence, thirteen is one plus three equals four. Do this with any other number and you will find that that number is, essentially, left alone; unchanged. In a sense you might say that nine, the number of God, exists *within* every other number. In addition to the translation from the Chaldean, or Semitic languages, to the western Greek and Latin tongues, numerology was, also, conceptually reframed. The modern system starts from the time of Pythagoras. Some claim that this is a result of spiritual and intellectual evolution. This sparked a strong debate as to which form was applicable and, to this day, there is still controversy in some philosophical circles. Since Herschel, or Uranus, was non-existent until 1781, seven planets and the Sun, hence the system of eight, were the only known astrological representatives. Since Saturn was, then, the outermost planet it represented the end of the known natural solar system. Currently, all the planets beyond Saturn are considered, in most circles, transpersonal and non-physical. To some numerologists, however, using the number of planets as a guide it would, now, make sense to work with a system of eleven since Neptune and Pluto have also been discovered since then. To prevent confusion I feel it's best to *not* include the modern nine based form of numerology in the sectioning off of the cycle and stay with the original eight based system.

Despite the controversy over number and letter correspondences, modern numerology, apart from the nine based format, does have a very solid and applicable reference to our exploration of cycles. Much like transiting Saturn and the progressing moon, numerology divides the Birth Path, or the main numerological lesson, into three sub-cycles. It does not distinguish between internal and external, as does the relationship between transiting Saturn and the progressing moon, but it does divide it into three twenty eight year cycles. The first is considered Formative, the Second is Productive and the third is the Harvest. These can also be considered physical, mental and spiritual, respectively. As transiting Saturn and the progressing moon may start the cycles at times different from exactly twenty eight years due to physical variations in their orbits, numerology contains similar possibilities for variations of up to five years. The beginning of each cycle is calculated by finding the nearest personal one year to twenty eight and fifty six years of age. Hence, the beginning of each cycle may start before or after the expected time frame.

With our general acquaintance with the three evolving periods in our awareness, let's return to the astrological format and fill in the twenty eight year cycle with a theoretical blueprint.

Who's LEADING the DANCE?
THE TIMING & THE INTERPLAY

Transiting Saturn and the progressing moon operate much like a mutual seesaw where our perception of and attitude toward circumstances (Moon) creates and encourages a reaction from the world (Saturn). In turn, the reactions of the world (Saturn) create and encourage our changing perspectives and opinions of it (Moon). These internal changes of opinion and perspective (Moon) create and encourage new and different reactions (Saturn). This is a karmic pendulum. This alternating continues ad infinitum until we recognize that we control *part* of the interplay. As we recognize our contribution to the reaction and react lesser toward an extreme, we lessen the length and intensity of the overall swing of the pendulum and gradually allow the perceived contradicting forces to fall closer into a balance.

It's also important to note that the natal and progressing moon *never* travels retrograde; however, transiting Saturn always does at least once per year. Due to this and the fact that the progressing moon travels faster on one side of the zodiac than the other, transiting Saturn and the progressing Moon, usually, do not change phase at exactly the same time. This says that on some phase changes we may feel an inner urge or "need" to follow the phase change due to the Moon arriving first and sometimes we may feel externally pressured to follow the phase when Saturn arrives first. The fact that Saturn (external) appears more erratic and that the Moon (internal) appears more consistent should be meditated on.

The alternating action between transiting Saturn and the progressing Moon is also a cycle in itself. Consider their relationship to each other much the same way that we view the changing tides, transition between day and night and any polarity where we can see perpetually alternating forces. Where awareness exists through the mind in our understanding is limited by the laws of rhythm and polarity and the continuity of time.

One last note; the descriptions may seem redundant as we describe the effects of transiting Saturn and the progressing Moon as they follow the same theoretical blueprint that the *transiting* Moon phases follow. However, it is important to note that the *transiting* Moon traverses each phase in a three and a half *day* period and transiting Saturn and the progressing Moon traverse each phase in a three and a half *year* period. The overall effect of these movements will be substantially less fleeting than that of the *transiting* Moon. This should also be meditated upon.

The CYCLIC PATTERN
IN 3.5 YEAR SEGMENTS

In the following descriptions please note that they are a theoretical representation only of what types of energy are in play in each of the phases. In Part 2 the descriptions are more tangible and specific to each age period as they are sequentially arranged as experiences, events and issues that are fairly common to the average population. Notice that I said *average* population. There are many individuals who follow a pattern that does not follow the most common path "of least resistance" typical to our culture. Marriages, births, career changes, special events may occur at times out of phase with the linear progression of expected growth and events. For those of you who fall into this group, it may be more difficult to perceive a clear picture of which phase you find yourself in.

The following is a linear progression of how the energies connect. They operate much like a row of dominos. The phases *always* follow one another consecutively. The perception of their occurrence out of order will be the result of mentally or physically backtracking to adjust the resulting conditions for the current phase. This should be seriously contemplated.

WAXING PHASES

EMERGENCE - 0-3.5 Years: (000-045 Degrees) – The cyclic perspective begins when transiting Saturn and the progressing Moon return to their place at birth the first, the second and possibly the third time at approximately 28, 56 and 84 years of age. What transiting Saturn and the progressing Moon manifest at birth is discussed in Part 2 of this book under the first twenty eight years of phases. What transiting Saturn and the progressing Moon bring with their first return is a full cycle of learning comprised of *what* life is as a balance between our "internal" or dharmic environment (the Moon and its progressions) and our "external" or genetic and karmic environments (Saturn's manifested world and our reactions). In that time we have gone through eight phases and established a format and perspective for dealing with the world.

For the first three and a half years of each cycle we start with what appears to be a blank slate for what ever new projects come into play with a prior programming from before the first cycle which gives us the tools that we will use to construct the new vision. As with the *emergence* Moon phase, there are no sign posts or guidelines externally and all we have to guide us is our internal vision of *how* we will use our accumulated "tools" to bring our vision into creation. This can be a very frustrating and insecure time for those of us whose self image is judged by the outcome of our efforts since trial and error are the only methods at hand. This feeling will also be exacerbated by issues produced in the first twenty eight year cycle that need resolution before the way is clear for the newer visions. When they are not answered they produce a blockage to the new energies; either through physical obstacles or emotional hesitations due to guilt, rebelliousness or unawareness. It's very much like attempting to build a house before the foundation has been properly settled. The causes for the incompleteness of a prior cycle can be produced by an illness, the birth of child, lack of awareness and many other factors including an unwillingness to acknowledge or be accountable for the prior precipitating circumstances.

However, this can be a very exciting time for those of us who enjoy the spirit of discovery and whose self image does not depend on the outcome of those new endeavors. There is a feeling of inspiration as visions and methods bubble up from our unconscious and intuition of new ways to handle old situations while producing new opportunities for bringing ones more fully expressive of our inner nature into being. Following the changes in this type of attitude is, essentially, traveling the road less traveled. The more we grow, the more we feel the urge to do so. It grows like a snowball rolling down the hill gathering momentum and materials. As we allow our intuition more expression, the creation seems to take on a life of its own.

It is important to note here that the progressing Moon and transiting Saturn follow, roughly, the same twenty eight year cycle. However, due the fact that the progressing Moon *never* retrogrades but that transiting Saturn does, it is likely that they will not change phase at the same time. If the Moon progresses to her birthplace before Saturn returns to his, our native may feel proactive with many of the urges toward new creations but not find the availability of circumstances in the physical world to apply those changes. They may find themselves "pushing the river" rather than being patient and allowing the right circumstances to fall into place first. Conversely, if Saturn returns to his place before the progressing Moon returns to hers, all the worldly conditions may be in place but the native may have difficulty understanding what to do with the opportunity or even realizing that it is the right time to act. Our native may appear to take on a more reactive perspective to physical conditions and events. In this light we can see that it is indeed fortunate and a blessing when both phases change at the same time.

The requirements to deal with this phase successfully are to, first, make certain that residual issues from the prior cycles have been appropriately addressed and handled and that, second, there is an awareness and a plan for where the new opportunities and energies are going to be applied. Once these actions have been completed we can, then, set the ground rules that operate in the next phase.

ASSERTION - 3.5-7 Years: (045-090 Degrees - Opening Semisquare) – The first three and a half years have been used in exploring parameters and learning a language that communicates our vision with and establishes the preliminary circumstances for our vision to manifest in the world. For every action taken or belief adopted, there is always someone somewhere who will disagree with the way we see or do things. In setting a focused course and in keeping with the laws of polarity, gender and rhythm, our energy will precipitate opposition. This will necessitate the clarification of the values and rules that we will use to sustain and promote the creation of our vision. These rules will constitute a path outlining the limits of fidelity to our endeavor. It is in this phase that we *choose* a belief system that will support our goal. Whether it is religious, philosophical, theoretical or Machiavellian, we assume that it will be the vehicle that will assist us. Essentially, this is where we establish a format or framework that provides the best environment for the growth of our project.

For astrologers it is also important to mention that because each phase consists of forty five degrees, the progressing Moon and transiting Saturn will change *sign* within each phase, on the average, once, possibly, two times, especially, when a sign is sandwiched between two change point cusps.

ACTION - 7-10.5 Years: (090-135 Degrees - Opening Square) – The action phase is a very tangible one. It is the most closely related to Aries and the Spring Equinox where growth or disintegration is the most visible and voracious. All of the energy is funneled into roughly structuring the physical manifestation of our project. This is also the phase at which Saturn is the least Saturnian in character and follows the more driven quality of Mars with the solid direction and determination of Saturn. It is not uncommon to feel as if the world is not adjusting fast enough to accept or meet the needs of our new creation. As our project takes shape, it's where the world gets its first glimpse of our coalescing dream as it emerges from the "cocoon" it's been incubating in. No one can assist in this growth, especially since it is not yet visible to the observer to allow them to know how to assist our creator. Hence, it may feel like one of the most frustrating and lonely phases of all, yet, the most exciting. This is the phase of the warrior.

EXPRESSION - 10.5-14 Years: (135-180 Degrees - Opening Sesquiquadrate) – The expression phase may be very subtle in its changes or overly expressive and exaggerated. Action has put our native's project into the world visibly. The responses that they receive confirm or deny how well it is measuring up to the world's expectations. Depending on the age and maturity of our subject, a need for notoriety and individualism may begin to surface. They may perform their daily tasks and actions with an eye for creating a unique presentation that will solicit an acknowledgement of the uniqueness of them and/or their creation. In this they may become hungry for an identity that "stands out."

Since this is the phase of the artist, it becomes one of the most individually creative phases of all. It's here that we begin to see the ingenuity of a focused mind and the flowering of artistic abilities. If our subject has grown in what might be considered a balanced emotional environment, these expressions will fall into step with innovations needed by our culture and will be, generally, welcomed and supported. If the emotional environment was one of "challenge," these expressions could take a more exaggerated and even violent form for the sole purpose of receiving acknowledgement as a worthy human being. For some, any attention is better than none. I believe that it is here where they are most likely to choose whether to follow a creative or destructive path in order acquire acknowledgement for their project.

WANNING PHASES

As we finish the first half of this cycle please remember that its focus has been one of construction and projection of the growing project. The first four phases "puts things in motion."

The need for the second half of this cycle, however, becomes increasingly more receptive in nature in order for growth and awareness to be activated and implemented. The last four phases present a need to now *yield* to the world's response to what has already been created. This shift in focus is extremely difficult for the typical westerner to adapt to. Westerners are accustomed to always taking an active role in any circumstance. Receptivity, letting go and listening are now needed.

Please note that it is important to remember that the focus and direction of the progressing Moon and transiting Saturn are both the same except for the fact that the Moon's phases (progressing) emanate from *within* our native and Saturn's movements (transiting) stimulate action that emanates from and creates *external* circumstances.

FULFILLMENT - 14-17.5 Years: (180-225 Degrees - Opposition) – This phase marks transiting Saturn's and the progressing Moon's first opposition or "full" phase: a milestone in growth on all levels. The fact that a full moon phase reflects the maximum possible light for awareness consciously *and* on the "shadow" or unconscious side of our subject's internal perspective is analogous to Saturn reflecting the fullest awareness of the structure our subject has created. At this point they literally begin to reap the "rewards and punishments" of what they have done, or not, thus far. It is a time of listening and looking back…if they are capable and/or allow themselves to do so. The hardest part, for any westerner, is to stop striving long enough to listen and take an "unbiased" look at what they have accomplished. Few people possess the ability to do so. At this time an impartial friend or counselor would be a help in enabling our subject to see themselves and their creation clearly.

Whether physically, emotionally or mentally, we all need support from the world to participate in it. Three different perspectives must be carefully integrated; first, the need to conform for acceptance, second, the need to create an individual identity with self respect and, third, acknowledging and accepting the fear of either being either swallowed, rejected or ignored by the world. Many factors contribute to the volatility of these energies, not the least of these is the native's chosen attitude as a result of passed experience. If our native is unable to accept the response they receive from the world relating to their creation, this and the following three phases will be made exceedingly difficult by their resistance toward accepting the world's judgment. They will feel that they must fight for every inch of acceptance. If our native recognizes the need to adjust their creation that it might fit into what the world requires, the remaining three phases will flow with a modest amount of effort. This phase is a critical turning point for the fate of our native and his project. These ages of change are easily recognizable as pivotal points in development. They are fourteen, forty two and seventy. Next to the *Assertion* phase, which established values, this phase is one of the most important for character revelation and development.

SYNTHESIS - 17.5-21 Years: (225-270 Degrees - Closing Sesquiquadrate) – Our native must take what they've created and integrate it with the needs of the social structure. This requires flexibility, adaptation, adjustment and, most of all, humility. The overwhelming need is for nurturance. Can our native switch gears from creating and leading to adjusting and supporting? Essentially, this is the native's first opportunity to sculpt their project into being accepted by the world on the world's terms. Bravado and identity enhancement are no longer needed or acknowledged and seen as an interference. How our native can support and augment the existing power structure with his creation becomes the deciding factor as to whether he will be allowed to share the benefits of that structure. The world is not interested in a new way of doing things unless it produces an advantage over prior methods. What useful qualities does the project bring? Can it be adapted to current needs? Flexibility and usefulness become of paramount importance. If our native's ego is substantially stable, then he or she will be able to keep their pride in check, acquiesce to the world's demands and gradually have a supported place in the world through the advantages their project brings. Those whose identities have not come into balance and still operate in a reactive mode will find themselves having limited or no access to support. The most obvious of those will, additionally, find themselves chastised and ostracized.

REORIENTATION – 21-24.5 Years: (270-315 Degrees - Closing Square) – The *synthesis* phase was the first indication of the need to let go of personal preferences in favor of the needs of the group in order to assure the continued support and maintenance of our native's desired life style. Now, there is a stronger need for a more visible sacrifice by them in order to be a more productive and accepted member of the group. The *synthesis* phase was more of a public probationary period to assess whether they could be trusted with maintaining the social structure already in place. Can our native comprehend the intended focus of that group and adapt his abilities, assets and patterns to contribute to its longer vision? In this frame it becomes much more obvious what components of the project must be released in order to meld with the overall vision. This is where they can develop superior listening skills by, consciously, putting their own needs and agenda on a back burner in favor of being patient in the building process. Delayed gratification becomes a much needed quality and, hopefully, its necessity becomes more noticeably obvious. As their listening becomes more pronounced, their social unity becomes more integrated. Of all the phases, this phase develops the highest degree of refined relationship qualities. Sharing becomes a dominant force and a growing asset. Conversely, this is also the point at which participation in a counter culture becomes much more pronounced for those who have opted not to work with the status quo. Those who connect with the counter culture only participate with the status quo in as much as it provides the basic necessities for survival. Essentially, both natives conform to a perspective either for or against the prevailing social vision. Either way, the *reorientation* phase exposes which perspective is supported.

RELEASE - 24.5-28 Years (315-360 Degrees - Closing Semisquare) – The overall focus of this phase is one of preparation for the coming new cycle. For the native who is aware of this, it only serves to increase the clarity of their life's purpose. For the ones who are not directly aware, it will still show itself through their acting on their intuition about what needs to be done. They will feel that they are, somehow, fated to a direction but not sure what it is. Whether conforming to the dominant culture or the counter culture the feelings of "destiny" will prevail as long as the native listens to their internal feelings. People in this phase have an uncanny ability to know what will come next for themselves and, with more clarity, for others based on the current observable circumstances. They can, sometimes, be prophetic with surprising accuracy. For the native who does *not* listen to their inner feelings this can be a very confusing time. They will feel that they are out of control and at the mercy of the changes in the environment. This phase will also create the feeling that nothing ever seems to come to a conclusion. It's as if everything is in the flux of preparation. What's most important to focus on in this phase is the necessity to give up or let go of patterns, people, careers, families and any influences that don't lend themselves to the creation of the pending new cycle. This can be done intentionally or through intuitive action for those who are aware. If awareness of the pattern is *not* present there can be losses that seem catastrophic and uncontrollable in the present but eventually, over time, become clear as having been necessary for change as future circumstances begin to unfold. The challenge of this phase is to learn to listen internally. As this occurs, outmoded patterns and circumstances begin to fall away or are consciously eliminated; their ability to cloud or obscure the life purpose becomes less pervasive. The "Path" that must be taken then becomes more obvious.

PART 2

What I have done thus far is to show the progression of perspective through different disciplines to give a feeling of the fullness and consequentiality in each of the cycles. Though the timing may be different, the essential patterns progress with the same propensity toward dove tailing and overlapping between sections. The "markers" between each "phase" are blurry at best and are often very difficult to ascertain, especially, where one ends and the other begins. We must remember that any method of division that we apply to a natural process, as I have with the eight phases, is purely arbitrary in the eyes of nature and applied merely to give our mind points of reference to perceive the continuity of our movement through past, present and future. In many other books of this nature what usually follows are concrete examples "empirically proving" and validating the hypothetical outlines through technical and detailed examples. Hence, we find life stories and circumstances quoted to show the connection to our lives through specific examples. My intention is not to "prove" a hypothesis but to present an opportunity to find our own point of development within the cycles that we may develop an intuitive blueprint on how to understand and proceed through our current place in our life process and to have a sense of where we will be going next. This process is *not* presented with the intention of labeling or judging our growth based on our position within each phase. This format is a "floating template" that depends on our *perceived* position in each cycle. How we perceive our point of development is solely dependent on our current state of awareness and can change in an instant depending on how we respond to new experiences as they present themselves. Additionally, when we assess our position we *must not* compare ourselves to others. We have no way of knowing, karmically, what someone has or hasn't been through yet. We all know what happens when we assume! Again, I am more interested in establishing the continuity of consequence rather than concretizing dates for change.

How to Use this Section
(for both astrologers *and* non-astrologers)

For those of you who are astrologers and would like to "pinpoint" the beginnings and endings of each phase it will be necessary to find the dates that transiting Saturn and the progressing Moon change phase through your ephemerides (for those of you who are not astrologers, this is a text containing daily positions of all the planets throughout specific years). If you know about Saturn transits (movements) and returns and Moon progressions, you know it is most likely that Saturn will pass a phase degree change point three times; once on the first transit, once on the retrograde transit and once on the direct transit and that the progressing Moon will pass it once. To establish exactly where the actual change takes place must include an analysis of the inner or faster moving planets, as they serve as initiators of visible action. As exact degree Saturn occurrences are rare at best we must accept Saturn's movement as only a backdrop or stage setter for the other planets to trigger visible circumstances. Please also remember that the progressing Moon follows the same cycle as Saturn but may produce effects internally before or after the actual physical Saturn transit. We must relegate ourselves to the understanding that each change is a gradual shifting of energy from one perspective to another. The best way to determine a specific time of shift is to use an experience that occurs within the time period as a beginning point.

For those of you who are *not* astrologers you must follow a different path to ascertain the change time and the phase you're working with. First, determine your age and find it in the section following. Read the section thoroughly. If it seems a good fit, you've found the phase you're working with. If it feels like you have already dealt with the issues being described, move *ahead* to the next age segment and, most likely, it will better portray your current experiences and feelings. If the section containing your age bracket feels unfamiliar to you, move *back* one phase and read that section. Odds are it will fit better.

Not everyone follows the same schedule of growth. Some of us change before the usual time and others of us change after. Some of us seem to be "late bloomers" and others seem to be "ahead of the game." Back to my initial admonition; DO NOT compare yourself to others and assess your growth as ahead of or behind others. Some of us first change *internally* before physical evidence presents itself (due to progressed moon changing before Saturn) and some of us change *externally* first and have to "catch up" with emotional adaptation (due to Saturn changing before the progressed moon). Neither is better or worse; just different. You may also change differently than your family does. Just because you may have hereditary tendencies does NOT mean you should be on the same schedule. Changing differently may be a lesson in itself.

Now that we have determined how to find the phase that is current, we will better recognize our current circumstances in terms of that phase and better understand our progression through this period in our lives. It gives us a framework and language to work with and talk about with others. Additionally, understanding the *following* phase will give us an edge on how to work with the current phase in order to initiate an easy flow into the following period. Planning will become easier and we will feel more confident in ourselves in knowing what we will be dealing with in the future. Looking at the *previous* phases will give us a more cohesive understanding as to why we might have had to experience issues the way we did.

It is important to note that one of the largest mitigating factors as to how the cycles will begin or "play out" is when the birth of children are introduced into the cycle. If they are introduced after the completion of the first twenty eight year cycle, the cyclic manifestations will appear in a fairly logical pattern and with continuity. If a child is introduced much before, as perhaps around twenty or twenty one, or at any other point other than the beginning of a cycle, the continuity of the twenty eight year cycle will be interrupted and visual evidence of the cycle's manifestations will seem to "loose the thread" of continuity making the pattern less obvious to the observer. This occurs because the native will usually lose awareness of their position in the cycle through being distracted in favor of attending the necessities and adjustments required to deal with the arrival of children. Their personal life goals and growth will most likely be "put on hold." If the birth, or even the acquisition of children through marriage, occurs close to twenty eight, as many do, or at about fifty six, the birth or acquisition will fall within the beginning new pattern and exhibit an obvious sense of continuity to the observer.

CYCLE I:
LEARNING

What a child comes into this life with is highly debatable as to qualities and character. If you support reincarnation it's easy to see that there is a need to balance the origin of characteristics between what a child brings in with it, what is learned and what is genetic after arriving. To differentiate between these three variables is difficult at best. If you don't support reincarnation, there are only two variables and you won't see it as an issue since it's assumed that all is either learned or genetic. I choose to believe that we arrive with some of the qualities in addition to what's learned and genetic and will proceed in this light.

Lastly, for astrologers, please remember that each aspect relates to both transiting Saturn and the progressing Moon.

Birth - 3.5 – Emergence Phase

Corresponds to:

New Moon – I Ching "K'an" – Birth Position – Yule – 000 Degrees

For the first three and a half years we start with what appears to be a blank slate. It is said by many that our personality is formed by age two. This would make sense from the perspective that a new born child is an empty vessel awaiting input. Consider a manufactured computer. It "comes into life" with a special type of programming tempered by its physical limitations of "inherited" structure. It utilizes the same type of power as every other computer and only develops unique and defining characteristics through encountering its own subjective environment and experience. The programming largely consists of energies developed in a "prior" existence. Its uniqueness and character is made obvious through how it handles the environmental circumstances presented to it. What isn't used, isn't seen...yet. Our prior programming relates to the Moon (dharma) and our environmental and genetic circumstances relate to Saturn (karma).

Imagine, if you can, being in an environment where all your physical needs are met, you're cuddled and gently "rocked" in, what seems to be, perpetual sleep. At some point something "erupts" in you and you find yourself pushing your way out of the womb and into the world. Where this urge comes from is, also, highly debated but occurs nevertheless. You're thrust into the cold, your food supply is cut off and you find yourself being moved about in all sorts of uncomfortable positions. Now, you are completely dependent on the "outside" world for peace, food and comfort. Your senses and feelings are completely overwhelmed and you have no understanding of how to replace the comforts you've lost. Suddenly, a nipple is placed in your mouth and you begin to suckle. You've just begun your relationship with the "external" world. The conscious awareness of Saturn has come into play. This starts the process of negotiating with the world. This is the first time you place your attention on anything outside of your own skin or even recognize that there is a difference. Boundaries are being established. It is now necessary to develop a way to communicate your needs. The responses you receive from the world start to build the patterns you will use for survival.

If you receive everything you need, you will come to expect the world to deliver it. From this point on you will look outside of yourself for your direction. You are now what we would consider externally motivated. If your needs are not met and you are not acknowledged, you will have to find a way to do it yourself. If you are no longer looking for an external response you will tend to become internally motivated. This seems to be very simple logic, right? Now, let's add the potential for the child bringing in a tendency for internal or self motivation. How will this child act in the face of receiving everything he or she needs? We can't tell. If the child comes in with an expectation of being taken care of by the outside world and receives no attention how will this child act in this instance? Again, we can't tell. The planets can only show *potential* for capabilities and types of action. They *cannot* predict what a living being will or won't do with that potential. So, can we predict what kind of child will grace the landscape based on anything in the chart? Yes. Can we predict what that child will do in any given situation? No. That is totally up to the child and how they integrate the energies and tendencies they bring in with the current hereditary and environmental circumstances. Unless we walk a mile in their booties we can never know!

At approximately two years Mars will return to its own place within the *Emergence* phase. A new pattern of action (Mars) will begin. The child will begin to test the boundaries to see how far they can go with manipulating their environment to meet their needs. Mothers and psychologists know this period as the "terrible twos." The sign that Saturn occupies tells what kind of limitations and structure the child will have to navigate through and the capabilities that will be developed as a function of that navigation. If Saturn changes sign before Mars returns to its place the child may temporarily lose his or her grounding (Saturn) and have to start again. This may not only confuse the child but the parent as well who may feel that the child appears to be acting out of character. As an example consider a child born with Saturn in Gemini and it changes to Cancer before Mars returns to its place. Where verbal cues (air) were once in force, it has now has switched to emotional ones (water). This requires a completely different type of comprehension on the child's part *and* the parent's part. The child may appear to almost be "set back" in his or her development. The child may be labeled as a "slow learner." From a karmic perspective, if any "prior programming" had need of being adjusted this would certainly be an effective way of accomplishing it.

It should also be noted that if the progressed Moon sign changes before Mars returns to its place the same intensity of confusion will take place however it will not be visible since the progressed Moon represents the inner urges (dharma). This change will be a lot harder to detect, let alone recognize and understand. However, seeing the change of sign will certainly give some clues.

From the child's perspective this is primarily a trial and error period colored by "preprogramming." From the parent's perspective this first phase is the most difficult and can be unbelievably nerve wracking since the child is, basically, unable to communicate what he or she needs. The urge to train is there for the parent but what is actually needed is patience and astute observation in order to see how the child is going to respond. Much like in a martial arts contest, we should never act until we see which way our "opponent" moves. To make the first move may miss vital information. We should, also, never assume that the child is going to act the way that we did at the same age.

3.5-7 – Assertion Phase

Corresponds to:

Crescent Moon – I Ching "Ken" – First Opening Semisquare – Imbolc – 45 Degrees

The first three and a half years have been used in exploring parameters and learning a language, actually and figuratively, that communicates with the world. To this point we have become cognizant enough to see patterns of the world as they connect to our survival. As a result, very slowly and painstakingly, we have moved toward developing behaviors to manipulate the world to serve us within those observed patterns. To do this we must form judgments about which actions work for us or not. We, then, commit ourselves to follow the ones that work for us. As we receive the world's response we choose a belief system that fits our perception of how things appear to us. Our mind begins to gain more and more control through its black and white discriminations and assessments of actions and events. We are becoming more invested in the physically polarized world. Our natural feeling nature is slowly becoming submerged as our ability to express it feels less and less tangible. It is becoming more difficult to communicate it as we recognize that the world will only deal with us through the static logic and reasoning quality of the language being learned. As a parent we begin to see the formation of a "solid" persona. Our child begins to assert him or herself. This includes what we perceive as "streaks of stubbornness" that are actually the child's attempt to adhere to a behavior that has attained results in the past.

At this point it is also important to mention that because each phase consists of forty five degrees, the progressing Moon and transiting Saturn will change sign within each phase, on the average, once, possibly, two times if a sign is sandwiched between two change point cusps.

7-10.5 – Action Phase

Corresponds to:

First Quarter Moon – I Ching "Chen" – First Opening Square – Ostara – 90 Degrees

The action phase is a very tangible one. At this point children tend to "shoot up" like string beans. Almost all of the energy is funneled into the body. Since their bodies are growing swiftly, developing coordination lags behind growth and they can seem extremely awkward and "gangly" in their movements. All physical action seems to be exaggerated. Independent action seems to be a necessity. More often we hear, "I'd want to do it myself!" If there is an interest in sports, it's now that it takes on intensity. There's more of a need to get "outside the house" and away from parents, restrictions and rules. The reactions and the responses they receive from parents and their peer group to the physical expressions of their independence develop profound effects on how much they will invest themselves into the outside world in the future. The influence of the material aspect of life takes on a profound importance. Intuition and the internal guidance system take a back seat to the required responses of the physical world. They become totally emulative of their heroes. Their ego and perception of themselves in the world takes on a tangible expression. At this point they have an idea of who they want to be and how they want to be seen. They act on the goals set for accomplishment that they believe will fulfill those imagined images of themselves. They act out in ways that imitate those personas with the expectations that they will validate their aspirations. It's when little boys act like firemen and policemen and little girls act like actresses and nurses; the prominent projected roles in life honored and admired by their parents and heroes. They innocently aspire to the projections of how those parents and heroes project how life *should* be. Being seen and not heard is no longer possible.

10.5-14– Expression Phase

Corresponds to:

Gibbous Moon – I Ching "Sun" – First Opening Sesquiquadrate – Beltane – 135 Degrees

The expression phase may be very subtle in its changes or overly expressive and exaggerated. Action has put the children in the adult world visibly. The responses that they receive confirm or deny how well they have measured up to the world's expectations and to their impressions of their heroes. After a time the world's approval is no longer enough to enable the child to form an expression that is individual and unique. They begin to fall into mediocrity with the rest of the population. There is nothing to distinguish them from anyone else. An urge for notoriety and individualism begins to surface. There develops a need to put their own twist to the responses that they apply to their experiences. They perform their daily tasks and actions with an eye for creating a unique presentation that will glean more notoriety and attention from those they had originally only attempted to imitate. They become hungry for an identity that "stands out." This phase becomes one of the most creative phases of all. It's here that we begin to see the ingenuity of the "new" mind and the flowering of artistic abilities. If a child has grown in what might be considered a balanced emotional environment these expressions fall into step with innovations needed by our culture and are, generally, welcomed and supported. If the emotional environment was one of "challenge," these expressions could take a more exaggerated and even violent form for the sole purpose of receiving acknowledgement as a worthy human being. In conjunction with these changes the physical body is developing more adult characteristics and the hormones of approaching puberty are producing a strong undercurrent of turmoil yielding, sometimes, an obsessive drive for personal recognition from the peer group to confirm or deny the accuracy of our budding adolescent's self appraisal. These changes in appearance also radically affect how uniqueness will be approached. In these years it is the most needed to have some sense of merging into the adult world. Right of Passage is necessary to show that acceptance into the adult world. Without it they are left to flounder with no understanding of their place or direction to take. I believe that it is here where they are most likely to choose whether to follow a creative or destructive path in order to establish a sense of identity.

As we finish the first half of this cycle please remember that its focus has been one of construction and projection of the growing persona. The first four phases "put things in motion." The need of the second half of this cycle, however, becomes increasingly more receptive in nature in order for growth to be activated and implemented. The last four phases present a need to *yield* to the world's response to what has already been created in body or in projects. This shift in focus is extremely difficult for the typical westerner to adapt to. Westerners are accustomed to always taking an active role in any circumstance. Receptivity, letting go and listening are now needed.

14-17.5 – Fulfillment Phase

Corresponds to:

Full Moon – I Ching "Li" – First Opposition – Litha – 180 Degrees

This phase marks the first opposition or "full" phase: a milestone in growth on all levels. The fact that a full moon reflects the maximum possible light on the "shadow" side of life is analogous to this phase reflecting the fullest awareness of the structure you have created up to this point. At this point you literally reap the "rewards and punishments" of what you have done, or not, thus far. It is a time of listening and looking back…if you are capable and/or allow yourself. The hardest part, especially at this age, is to stop striving long enough to listen and take an unbiased look at what you have, thus far, accomplished. Few adolescents possess the ability to do so. Generally, parents, teachers and stewards fill this role. Even *they* must hold back and allow you enough room to respond and come to your own conclusions. The temptation to *tell* you what has been happening and how to respond is overwhelming, especially, if your parents feel insecure about their own choices and current identities. If your parents are unable to refrain from doing so, the development of your necessary self assuredness gained from self exploration will be blocked from growing. You will then be hopelessly lost in looking for personal direction from the *outside* world rather than from your own internal dharma. This contributes to the momentum of the reactive mind and diminishes creativity. The lion you could have been might turn into a sheep. This phase of life corresponds to balancing how much of life must be adhered to based on performance and how much can be pursued through personal creativity and interest. You need support from the world in order to participate in it. Three different perspectives must be carefully integrated; your need to conform for acceptance, especially, with your peer group, your need to create an individual identity with self respect and, last, the fear of either being swallowed or ignored by the world. Many factors contribute to the volatility of these energies. The most important of these are home environment, heredity, diet, education, participation and your individual experience. Here your choices are crucial to determining your attitude toward the world and yourself for the rest of your life. Next to the *Assertion* phase, which established values, this phase is the most important in your character development.

17.5–21 – Synthesis Phase

Corresponds to:

Disseminating Moon – I Ching "K'un" – First Closing Sesquiquadrate – Lughnasad – 225 Degrees

"Coming of age" is an important time in that now you must take what you have learned and become and begin to integrate it, and yourself, into the social structure. The hardest point in the cycle, for your western mind, is learning to listen to and accept how the world assesses you. This requires you to focus outside of your usual personal perceptive frame. Not only must you look for feedback about how you project on the world but you must seek an understanding of how it will be used by others and why. In practicing this you will begin to heighten your receptive qualities by learning to listen with a sense for what is needed by others that you may both feel supported and unthreatened. In a sense, you are learning how to nurture your new "larger family." Hopefully, you will find, as a "byproduct," that listening and perceiving where to apply conscious service helps you to develop qualities of gentleness, nurturance, submissiveness, devotion and "unconditional" sensitivity which must be formed, or at the least recognized, if you are to survive and gain support from the world. Essentially, you must participate on the world's terms. Bravado and identity enhancement are no longer needed or acknowledged except as an interference. Adapting and humility are now required. How you can support and augment the existing power structure becomes the deciding factor as to whether you will be allowed to share the benefits of that structure. The world is not interested in a new way of doing things, especially, from the voice of your inexperience no matter how creative you may be. What qualities do *you* bring to *their* new social experience? Can your skills and experiences be adapted to the world's current needs? Flexibility and usefulness become of paramount importance. If your identity has been successfully developed you will be able to keep your pride in check, acquiesce to the world's demands and gradually gain access to power in the world. Those of you whose identities have not come into balance and still participate in the reactive mode of adolescence will find yourselves having no access to any positions of power at all. The most obvious of you will, additionally, find yourselves being chastised and ostracized. In this phase, you will also develop internal tension over your choices between peer groups and elders. Becoming a bridge between the two can be a tremendous asset in that it exhibits your potential leadership qualities and personal initiative to those in power, however, this can sometimes, also, be seen as a threat depending on the security of those in power.

21-24.5 – Reorientation Phase

Corresponds to:

Third Quarter Moon – I Ching "Tui" – First Closing Square – Mabon – 270 Degrees

The *synthesis* phase was the first indication of the need to let go of personal preferences in favor of the needs of the group in order to assure the continued support and maintenance of your desired life style. Now, there is a stronger need for a more visible sacrifice by you in order to be a more productive and accepted member of the group. The *synthesis* phase was more of a probationary period to assess whether you can be trusted to maintain the social structure already in place. Can you comprehend the intended focus of that group and adapt your abilities, assets and patterns to contribute to its longer vision? The keywords here are adjustment, cooperation, revamping and tailoring. You may be aware of the parts of your social group that you fit well with but you are, also, painfully aware of where you do not. This is where you can develop more superior listening skills by, consciously, putting your own needs and agenda on a back burner in favor of being patient in the building process. Releasing personal expectations becomes a deeper and more compassionate step for you toward the required letting go. Delayed gratification becomes a much needed quality for you to develop and, hopefully, its necessity will become more noticeably obvious to you. As your listening skills become more pronounced, your social skills will become more adept. Of all the phases, this phase develops the highest degree of positive and negative relationship qualities. Sharing should be becoming a dominant force and a growing quality within you. This is also the point at which the tendency toward choosing to participate in a counter culture becomes much more obvious to the observer for those of you who have opted not to join the status quo. Those of you who connect with the counter culture will only participate with the status quo in as much as it will provide the basic necessities for your survival. Essentially, both of you will conform to a perspective either for or against the prevailing social structure. Either way, the *reorientation* phase exposes which perspective either of you chooses to conform to.

24.5-28 – Release Phase

Corresponds to:

Balsamic Moon – I Ching "Ch'ien" – First Closing Semisquare – Samhain – 315 Degrees

The overall focus of this phase is one of preparation for the coming new cycle. As a new adult who is aware of this, this only serves to develop an observable clarity and awareness of your life's purpose. For those of you who aren't, it will still show itself, though less obviously, through your acting solely on your intuition about what needs to be done. You will feel that you are, somehow, fated to a direction but not sure what it is. Whether conforming to the dominant culture or the counter culture, the feelings of "destiny" will prevail as long as you listen to your internal feelings. While you are in this phase you have an uncanny ability to know what will come next for yourself and, with more clarity, for others based on the "feel" of the current observable circumstances. You can, sometimes, be prophetic with surprising accuracy. For those of you who do *not* listen to your inner feelings, this can be a very confusing time. You will feel that you are out of control and at the mercy of the changes in the environment. Being accountable and responsible for the consequences of your actions, rather than feeling like a victim who is inclined to blame others, can become a strong mitigating factor against your feeling helpless and contribute to a more proactive approach in tackling life's challenges. Yet, this phase will also create the feeling that nothing you participate in ever seems to come to a conclusion. It's as if everything is in a flux of preparation. This is also a common and appropriate time to consider a career change, marriage or a plan for having children. This shows you the necessity of making and keeping goals in mind in order to promote the continuity of your assessed purposes. What's the most important to focus on in this phase is the necessity to give up or let go of patterns, people, careers, families and influences that don't lend themselves to the formation of the pending new cycle. A positive side effect of doing this produces an added availability of energy as each outmoded behavior is given up, thereby, reducing the drain on the personal energy that was used to keep it in place. Now, the freed energy can be used for more constructive applications. Again, this can be done by you intentionally and with awareness or through intuitive action by those of you who are unaware. If you have no awareness of the pattern, losses can seem catastrophic and uncontrollable in the present but eventually, over time, become clear as having been necessary for change as future circumstances begin to unfold. The challenge of this phase is to learn to listen and act on your internal voice and not look for external validation. This can be extremely difficult to do, especially for those of you who have been trained to only look to external authority for guidance about what is right or wrong. When you learn to do this, your outmoded patterns and circumstances will begin to fall away and their ability to cloud or obscure your life purpose will become less pervasive. The "Path" that must be taken will then become more obvious.

CYCLE II:
PRODUCTION

Until now you have been learning who you are, what you are capable of and how the world will react to what you present to it. Marriage and life changes now have the best potential for success since you have, hopefully, successfully navigated through and gotten a taste of all eight phases at least once. How quickly internal indicators are perceived by you will determine how soon your major changes will actually take place. Generally, they occur somewhere between twenty seven and twenty nine years of age. In these years you will most likely see the arrival first born children, pivotal career choices and life path focuses with the most lasting effects.

28-31.5 – Emergence Phase

Corresponds to:

New Moon – I Ching "K'an" – First Return – Yule – 000 Degrees

New experiences take on a different color than the previous *emergence* phase. You now have a full sense of self, though not necessarily accurate, and an urgency to make your mark on the world with your own personal brand of creativity. Like the first *emergence* phase you are leaping into the void and the unknown except, this time, you have a personal history to use as a guide for future choices. The challenge you feel provides both fear and excitement as it is triggered by the darkness of your internal guidance and intuition. It feels exhilarating and terrifying all at the same time. Everything is new. Everything has promise. You perceive everything as being possible. The feeling of knowing something of the world and yourself fuels an ever expanding feeling of hope within you. You now have the ability to look back and see the choices that you have made that have most poignantly contributed to your current life circumstances. Like the *release* phase just before, intuition is the prime guiding force except instead of sensing *where* to take new action you must step back *after* the action is taken and listen for your internal reaction. Essentially, this is a time of "trying on" new perspectives and getting a feel for them relative to choosing your new path. The most intimidating factor of this type of "experimentation" or trial period is the possibility of not being able to reverse an action that you choose to take. You can change your career or where and how you live many times with minor complications; however, bringing a child into the world is one of the only exceptions that is irreversible. Since there are no external signposts and no one to ask for directions in this phase, your challenge is to develop concentration, focus and a sense of listening within to allow the vision of the future to penetrate your awareness fully. The ability to do this might be considered one of the most beneficial consequences of cultivating a sense of "innocence."

31.5-35 – Assertion Phase

Corresponds to:

Crescent Moon – I Ching "Ken" – Second Opening Semisquare – Imbolc – 045 Degrees

Now that you have "tried on" a pattern and found it to your liking, you must now set plans as to how these choices will be filled out. This is a time of committing to the choices that you have made. Your plans will illustrate the depth and seriousness of those commitments. It's a time of affirmation. However, this is not the type of affirmation "buzzed" by the metaphysical world leading to a self-deceptive expectation that the goal will magically manifest without the application of any practical effort. It *is*, however, one of declaring your intentions to others, openly, so that others may feel secure in what they might expect in terms of structure and support from you. In a sense it is a kind of contract you are making with the world. Fulfilling it, in the world's eyes, is confirming any trust that it may have invested in you. Yet, there is more here than meets the eye. As we grow in awareness we begin to understand that actions and choice are multileveled in their effects. In this case, there is a very important factor which, usually, for most of us, exists below the threshold of awareness. The commitments we make represent the choices we have made and will take action on consciously but they also reflect the opportunities we have *not* taken and lost as possibilities. The Chinese say, "By choosing the fruit we discard the chaff." In this, any choice, no matter how large or small, closes off the availability of what is *not* taken. The fear of losing options is one of the major reasons contributing to "fear of commitment" as it is known today. Understanding and accepting that you "can't have it all" shows wisdom in dealing with the world. Lastly, to commit to a path or a belief will precipitate conflicts of interest or, at the worst, enemies. This is one of the down sides of committing to anything. There is always someone who will oppose what you do, want or believe. In this, the risk of selling out to maintain your social "safety" becomes a very real concern. The second most important reason for "fear of commitment" is the threat of confrontation and of being ostracized. Even in light of these circumstances, full commitment to any clear cut goal can focus a tremendous amount of energy, momentum and potential and builds your courage and self confidence for dealing with future challenges and choices. Which way you respond will be seen by the world as a test of your character.

35-38.5 – Action Phase

Corresponds to:

First Quarter Moon – I Ching "Chen" – Second Opening Square – Ostara – 090 Degrees

With a focused path, a clear plan and a commitment, this phase, usually, produces dramatic results in the visible world. Remembering that this phase is the most physical, it's no wonder that we see the most tangible evidence of growth in your home, career and family. Whether that growth is seen as a success or a disaster it is, still, the most volatile of all the phases. The risk here is that your tendency toward shear force, action and momentum will outstrip your ability to keep hold of the reins tightly enough to stay in control. The requirement is akin to guiding a tidal wave in the right direction. You may feel so driven toward success, almost to the point of ruthlessness, that anything and anyone standing in your way risks obliteration. You have almost a warrior mentality that focuses on purging the old and forging the new with lightning action. This can be a very physically challenging time for you so it's important to make certain that your nutritional needs are met or even surpassed. You may also have the tendency to overextend yourself; physically harming yourself or putting yourself in circumstances which you are unable to navigate effectively due to over confidence or lack of foresight. During this time compassion may not be high on your priority list. There is such an outer directed energy that listening may be all but lost. As long as you can share the focus of your drive with another person, perhaps a spouse, there will be open communication. If your drives feel unanswered or unaddressed, you may feel hard pressed to make yourself heard or to make a point to your partner. You will feel a sense of feeling "stuffed" and lost in the shuffle with no place to invest your tidal wave of energy. If your energy is not invested in *something* constructive it will most certainly find its way into destructive behavior; either toward your spouse or toward yourself. It is important to note that destructive behavior, especially repressed, *always* contributes toward illness whether it is physical, emotional and/or mental. Inception of this type of illness has a gestation period before it becomes visible to the external world. It builds pressure and manifests over a long period of perseverant imbalanced emotional patterning; first, coalescing in the mental, then expanding into the emotional and, finally, manifesting into the weakest part of your physical body. If your energy *does* have an avenue for expression there is tremendous potential for your creativity and for you having an effect on the world.

38.5-42– Expression Phase

Corresponds to:

Gibbous Moon – I Ching "Sun" – First Opening Sesquiquadrate – Beltane – 135 Degrees

If you have been successful in putting your plans into action there is now a rudimentary framework available for future embellishing. Hopefully, at this point, most of the major distractions, such as the survival of your self and your family, has been handled or, at least, relegated to a comfortable and competent pattern for minimizing the amount of energy invested in their handling. The task now is to "fill in the blanks" and give the project(s) beyond survival your personal signature. This phase is one of the most creative and innovative. At this point, there has been so much energy invested your current projects that any modifications and adjustments easily flow along with their momentum. This is where you might start acting and looking like your mom and dad. Personal creations, our children included, are taking on your uniquely personal characteristics. Your professional changes exhibit the style and the characteristics typical of you as their author. Everything that has been done in the previous phase begins to take on its own unique coloring. This is the phase of the actor, the artist, the musician, the writer and any activity that will lend itself toward enhancing the image and personal expression of you the author. For the current projects this is the last opportunity to "improve" upon them. It is here that their "fate" is sealed and how they will appear in history. Your actions here will color and classify your expression in the eyes of the current social structure and lead toward being labeled and associated with specific groups and their characteristics. In a sense, it builds and strengthens your connections to and rejections by your families; whether personal or career. The danger here lies in the motivation behind your actions. Are you accomplishing strictly for recognition or do your intentions go beyond your personal image? All of us want the acceptance and the approval of the groups and individuals that we admire and hold in reverence. But at this point you must ask what the limit is to which you will extend yourself in order to acquire that? This phase will most clearly expose the intensity of your need..

42-45.5– Fulfillment Phase

Corresponds to:

Full Moon – I Ching "Li" – Second Opposition – Litha – 180 Degrees

This phase is probably the most crucial to our learning how to handle life. In astrology there are, essentially, four transits happening at the same time. First, Uranus opposes its natal position. Second, transiting Saturn and progressing Moon oppose their natal positions for the second time and, third, Neptune squares its natal position. Both oppositions are aspects of awareness. Here you begin to reassess your history and potential. Whether you are willing or not is not an option. It occurs either way. You may address the process or repress it. It happens nevertheless. You can view your life with satisfaction, regret or a mixture of both. This is not only a time where you must accept and acknowledge your progress thus far but you must also allow others to offer their assessments and judgments that you may have a clear understanding of how you fit, or not, into the current social scheme of things. The hardest part or this process, especially for westerners, is ceasing construction and the application of effort and energy to any life project and allowing yourself to be receptive to the response of the world. In short; it will be hard for you to "let go."

When you are satisfied with your accomplishments, you are led to planning their expansion that they may become self perpetuating in order to sustain you in later years. You have a sense of identity that has been created leading to a feeling of pride and assurance of your position in whatever life style you have established. Friends and business associates reflect the quality of this identity. Your life has a sense of certainty and a feeling that you are on an accelerated path toward a desired destiny. You approach life with energy and confidence.

When you assess your life and you have *not* accomplished what you wanted to, you can handle it in two ways. First, you can be honest with yourself and make some hard choices by redressing your goals from a different perspective and then mustering up the courage and passion to reengage the battle. This involves the very difficult task of recognizing and letting go of some of your beliefs that have led you to this position in life without the intended accomplishments. In doing this you must be careful not to chastise yourself for not having the foresight that your hindsight has now brought you. Beating yourself up accomplishes nothing except to reinforce the disappointment. You must not judge *yourself* but instead, judge your *behavior* as being misdirected. The key here is not to take it personally. The fault you assess is NOT in your character but in your methods. As you choose your methods based on your beliefs you, also, choose your beliefs based on your experience. If you choose a different belief to operate by, you can create a different experience. Every belief begins as an initial choice of action, becomes substantiated as your experience through the world's reaction to it and, after repeated occurrences, becomes a habit. This creates your expectations for the future. If the reaction is not what you have intended, this becomes a vicious cycle. Breaking the cycle becomes crucial to changing your life experience and expectations. The old adage says, "If we do what we have always done, we will get what we have always gotten." Second, if you *cannot* be honest with yourself, by whatever reason you tell yourself, you're in a different kettle of fish. To bury the discomfort of the resurfacing assessment you may take actions designed to mask or overshadow its effects. For example, men may distract themselves with acquiring toys such as motorcycles and the lifestyles that accompany them, especially, if they have been fairly conventional throughout their lives. Women may begin dating younger men so they may get lost in the excitement and inexperience of youth. Whatever action is chosen for either sex, the intention is to avoid dealing with the reality of the assessment. Like excessive alcohol use, a hangover is inevitably going to lead back to the reality of what was avoided on the morning after. The motorcycles and the younger men may take a bit longer but there always is, inevitably, a return to the stark reality of the original assessment. Some clues as to how a person will react can sometimes be surmised by examining the types of choices that were made when the first opposition occurred at fourteen. The saddest cases of avoided assessments lead to self destructive behavior. Some of the more extreme cases never recover.

Neptune's square to its natal position is a new event and focus. It operates at, literally, a different frequency from the inner individuality of Uranus and the progressing Moon and the practical outer material world of Saturn. It is more akin to the emotional world of the progressing Moon. The struggle between your inner world and your outer world is no longer as clear as it had been in the past. The struggle is now three sided. Confusion sets in with the arrival of the possible existence of an energy or force of awareness comprised of much more than your own perceptions and actions. In this light you begin to look at your mortality and whatever beliefs you hold pertaining to the spiritual content of what you have done thus far. Please understand that when I refer to "spiritual" I mean that which exists simply beyond the physical, the logical and the every day mundane. Do not assume that the currently held unilateral perspective of New Age thought composes its building blocks. It is composed of many more layers and dimensions. Even there, there is the possibility of self deception; a ripe target for Neptune's dissolving energies. It can include religion if it is founded on real working principles but is not limited to it. In this day and age there are many religious lifestyles that would not withstand the nature of Neptune's "reality check." Neptune embodies the character of a "dissolver" of whatever it affects or touches, but only that which has a shaky foundation or a deceptive nature. Beyond that it possesses the potential for the refinement and fine tuning of whatever it touches. Artistic talent can ascend to fantastic heights or plummet to the deepest, darkest part of egotistical delusions and twisted, self deceptive embellishments. Much like the sculpting perspective of Michelangelo, Neptune dissolves away the outer layers to reveal the shape and the character of the essential sculpture within. This process can take anywhere from five years or more merely to approach the understanding of what it is producing. Once there is that awareness, midlife becomes the point of no return with a clearer view of the struggle.

45.5-49 – Synthesis Phase

Corresponds to:

Disseminating Moon – I Ching "K'un" – Second Closing Sesquiquadrate – Lughnasad – 225 Degrees

If you have been able to stop production and take time to listen, you are beginning to get an understanding of how your actions and assets may be of use to the world. This is the phase where what is required for success is to be primarily selfless in order to move with the natural pattern of the cycle. By this age your children are now having children and you must work to streamline your accomplishments so that they may be of use to your extended family and others and abandon any need to apply a personal signature to your projects. It is no longer about you but what your personal world and the world at large needs from you to run smoothly. Your projects must be transformed into something that nurtures the world even at the expense of your social image. The key qualities to promote this are humility, adaptation and usefulness. Not everyone is going to be able to use or appreciate your accomplishments. Your concern should be for what you can do to make them more accessible, enjoyable and useful to others. If you are still mired in a need for recognition, this time will produce a "crash and burn" for you. You must accept the fact that the more homogeneous you make your accomplishments, the more useful they will be to everyone else, however, they will, necessarily, retain less for your personal recognition. To integrate your creation into the flow of your natural social structure would give the best complement as to its usefulness. This action would also answer the need for the nurturing part of your nature to emerge. The requirement here is of blending, education and, most emphatically, the elimination of egotistical pride as related to your project. By this time you should *already* possess a strong sense of self thereby eliminating the need to project an image that builds your pride. During this time it would not be uncommon for you to tutor or mentor younger adults in their struggle to create the projects that you have already accomplished.

49-52.5 – Reorientation Phase

Corresponds to:

Third Quarter Moon – I Ching "Tui" – Second Closing Square – Mabon - 90 Degrees

Having worked to adjust what you have created to be of use to others you are also aware of what parts of your accomplishments have outlived their usefulness. To maintain these parts would be to waste valuable energy that you could apply to developing new trends. You must withdraw this energy and let go of any personal attachments to your accomplishments. This also means turning over the reigns of control to the up and coming generations. You must further refrain from mentoring and let your fledglings "peddle without training wheels" on their own. Your instinct will be to either help them or do it for them to maintain your feeling of usefulness. This may be conscious or unconscious but, nevertheless, must be undertaken. On some level you are instinctively aware that there is a new cycle developing for you and that this severing is your first preparation for it. Also, what has become painfully apparent, are the goals that you have set for yourself early on that have never materialized. When you were younger you saw yourself as having a broader scope of effect on the world around you. You saw yourself as being much more important to the world than is the case in the reality of things. You see some of your past goals as no longer having the potential or the time left needed for their creation. You begin to see a necessity for investing your energy into your family and close friends that they may accomplish what you no longer have the longevity left to follow through. However, you must be extremely careful not to allow yourself to *expect* that they will want to complete what you have started. The urge for your progeny to carry on your work may be overwhelming, especially, if it stems from an unconscious need. You must allow them to make their own choices and know that their path may move in a very different direction from your original intentions. You begin to see your significance *and* insignificance in the world at large. You can no longer look at the reality check that you took in the *fulfillment* phase as a *possibility* for non-completion or unrealized projects but as likelihood. With this understanding, your mortality draws closer. Your questions move toward what might be beyond this tangible world. If you can accept the fact that you must let go of "here" you may become comfortable with the questions about "there." If not, you may become obsessed with the need that your work must be carried on in a way that extends the proliferation of your individuality. Ego is the antithesis to being at peace.

52.5-56 – Release Phase

Corresponds to:

Balsamic Moon – I Ching "Ch'ien" – Second Closing Semisquare – Samhain – 45 Degrees

At this point in the cycle you begin to feel the positive effects of letting go of old finished patterns. The process of letting go accelerates as you begin to feel the power in being free from your past goals and aspirations. As you let go, the new cycle begins to unveil itself and you begin to gain more of an understanding of the purging that must take place in order to accommodate the new cycle. With this you start to see the possibilities and end results of the patterns people around you are adhering to. An uncanny ability to see the future of current choices and circumstances, for others, makes you feel like you are more psychic than observant. People you communicate this with may find you a bit eerie but are drawn to you nevertheless; much like a sooth sayer would attract the curious. It's a strange place to be; not belonging to the current world of patterns but not quite connected to the "new" one. This phase is the same as when the Moon is void of course. There, you have no apparent direction or anchor, especially, since the new direction has not been tangibly defined. It's as if you're standing on the edge of the abyss with nothing to hold on to. Can you trust yourself? Your direction is only "felt" by you as the "right" or "wrong" place to go or be. It's totally intangible and intuitive. This situation creates and strong feeling for and opportunities to practice listening to the small voice inside which tends to dramatically hone your skill.

CYCLE III:
ESTABLISHING BALANCE

For most of the two earlier cycles you have been participating from a more reactive perspective than proactive. More appropriately put, you have been reacting from within the limits of your early externally motivated conditioning training to respond to an external authority. You were trained as to how you were to behave and act if you wanted approval and support from the world at large. Within this training was a tacit message encouraging you to believe that if you "worked hard" in the way dictated by the delegated authority (remember, you delegated it to them) that you would be "successful" and that your security needs would be met. Whether the intention of this was conscious or unconscious, it was, nevertheless, a misconstrued myth manipulating the young into servitude and providing the safety of the status quo for those in authority. As you grew to experience more of the world you have come to understand that the only approval and support you could count on was your own and that "the only security there is is knowing that there is none" (Alan Watts). Slowly you shifted from being responsive to and motivated by *externally* generated rules and goals to being responsive to and motivated by *internally* generated feelings, intuition and creativity. The older you get and the more internally motivated you become, the more others begin to see you as eccentric, cantankerous, "unruly" and unwilling to follow the "rules" as outlined by your early conditioning.

At midlife a shift occurs. You begin to become *more* internally motivated but this change happens very gradually through many years and experiences. The relationship that exists between internal and external motivation is a reciprocal one.

That is, as one type of focus increases the other decreases and vice versa; much like the shift between day and night; gradually. If you consider how a mortgage operates it, generally, has a thirty year life span. In the beginning you pay mostly interest but at the end you're paying mostly principle. The shift happens at fifteen years, at which point, the payments to each are equal but then shifts in the opposite emphasis. In the same fashion you fulfill your eighty four year life expectancy in the same way. For the beginning of the first half of life until forty two you live within the limits of your early external conditioning. Beginning at forty two, or midlife, you gradually begin to lean more heavily into your own preference, experience and volition. What others think of you becomes less of a concern to you. At this age you begin to feel you've seen it. You've done it.

The older you become the more the effect of your early conditioning diminishes. Your direct experience and accumulation of understanding, now encouraging you to live by your own volition and preferences, is overtaking the need to be concerned as to how others see and approve of you. Through your early conditioning you were led to believe that it was extremely important that the world perceived you as a contributing member and, thereby, "deserving" of its approval and support. You believed that your image and how people perceived you was the strongest contributing factor as to how you "should" see and assess yourself and that that would be what fulfilled your need for security. Toward the latter half of life, for most of you whose material needs and abilities have become actualized, your understanding grew in a different direction. You came to understand that those who have conditioned you to need them, need you, just as much as you felt you needed them; a symbiotic relationship. Changes in symbiotic relationships happen reciprocally while maintaining a balance. If not, the relationship ends and you look for someone else to fulfill the new complimentary role dictated by the change. Everyone has to adjust. Additionally, your focus has shifted from what you *need* from others to what you feel you *want* to give them. You have realized that your contributions were just as important as those in power.

With these perspectives in mind let's continue on our journey into the last and most dynamic cycle.

56-59.5 – Emergence Phase

Corresponds to:

New Moon – I Ching "K'an" – Second Return – Yule – 000 Degrees

If you have been able to let prior conditioning fall by the wayside this can be the beginning of a tremendously creative period. As with the previous phases, this phase requires you to take your direction from your internal compass rather than from external social signposts, especially which, in this phase are virtually non-existent. However, since a proactive internal motivation has been slowly increasing to overtake your early reactive conditioning, listening to the small voice within has been becoming increasingly easier. This coupled with your own maturing opinions of what values you feel *should* be adhered to, provides a fertile foundation and ability to create from your own individual form of expression unhindered by social demands and requirements. In its most dramatic form of expression this could show as preponderance toward genius or; in its least, eccentricity. This is not to say that you have given up responding to the social demands created by your conditioning to insure your survival but that there is more of a blending of what is *preferred* for your creativity as opposed to what behavior is *required* to maintain the quality of life you feel is appropriate for you. What is so beautiful about this phase is the opportunity for unleashing your intuitive expression. This, essentially, has the effect of quieting the mind and augmenting the spirit. At this point you, hopefully, have learned that the chattering mind is a function of your continuing struggle to reconcile external demands with internally generated preferences. Meditation then becomes the best key to balance, and is made easier due to the fact that you are less concerned with your responsiveness to your environment. This phase is the representative for your most dynamic unfettered intuitive action which is still the requirement for you to actualize your next creative project. The importance of this phase is that it not only makes this task easier by freeing you from outdated traditions but, lays the framework for how you will live life for the next twenty eight years.

59.5-63 – Assertion Phase

Corresponds to:

Crescent Moon – I Ching "Ken" – Third Opening Semisquare – Imbolc – 45 Degrees

If there is no difficulty determining *where* to put you creative energy, setting a plan as to *how* you are to achieve your goals is extremely easy. At this age you are fairly strong and certain of your values so there is no contest as to what your priorities are in their importance. All that is left is to choose the methods you'll use. If you are compassionate there may be some concerns as to the needs and desires of others but if you are driven there might be little consideration. To one who is of a Machiavellian nature, this is a "piece of cake." To someone with a conscience, it will take some careful planning so as not to step on anyone's toes. At sixty there is, also, a fairly good understanding of how the "conventional" world works. Hence, if there is outside support needed to accomplish your objectives it should be fairly easy to know where to rally it from. Additionally, since you have experienced and seen a great deal of life, the urgency to complete the task, in the fear that an opportunity will be missed due to inexperience or unawareness, is absent. There is a more relaxed approach and you can create a plan that is well grounded and practical. This creativity will also be applied to your anticipated retirement if you are able to retire.

63-66.5 – Action Phase

Corresponds to:

First Quarter Moon – I Ching "Chen" – Third Opening Square – Ostara – 90 Degrees

This is where you will see the most physical evidence of the shift that has taken place over the last seven years. However, this evidence will appear to be, to the observing world, less obvious than what was exhibited in the prior two cycles. Since the urgency of youth has been tempered by the experience of age, you have more of a feeling of being content with whatever the world will allow in terms of that creativity. This phase, in the prior two cycles, intense in the first and more moderate in the second, was much like holding on to a wild horse rocketing into the unknown. The phase energy of this third cycle is much more channeled, directed and consistent than the prior two. You have, also, more of an acceptance and trust as to where the horse is going. You have more confidence that you can handle whatever the world may "throw at you" and you are more confident in knowing the pertinent facts that will contribute toward the successful accomplishment of your new goals.

Provided your health is still in good shape, the energy directed here will be focused, consistent and almost impervious to outside interference. You will also have a salient understanding of what is actually possible under the prevailing circumstance. You, also, have more of an astute understanding about timing with a deeper wisdom about when to be patient and wait and when you can push forward. Unless maturity has stagnated, this period will show a marked absence of the need for immediate satisfaction which is so common in youthful inexperience.

66.5-70 – Expression Phase

Corresponds to:

Gibbous Moon – I Ching "Sun" – Third Opening Sesquiquadrate – Beltane – 135 Degrees

As your new goals begin to take shape in their rudimentary form, this becomes more of a time of refining their effectiveness rather than making them a statement of your uniqueness. With maturity your need for the approval and the "wowing" of others is relatively absent. This allows you to focus your energy more uniformly without being scattered by conflicting objectives much like the single-mindedness of a child who has not yet become susceptible to conflicting needs for approval. This challenge for expression comes as an effort to mold your creativity in a form that most clearly manifests your originally conceived vision as was seen and felt in the peak of your clarity. Its reception by others is much less important than the clarity of its reflection of what you see and feel inside.

There also occurs an opportunity for change in the expression of your sexuality. The first *Expression* phase occurs at puberty when hormones are raging. At that age they most often fuel either the need to prove something or an irresistible curiosity. The second time occurs just before midlife. This, in itself, is a turbulent time for confirming or redefining who you are. Here too sexuality is a very large part of the landscape and takes the form, if not just for pleasure, as either your need for recognition or the confirmation of your identity through the responses of others. In this third *Expression* phase it takes a completely different coloring. Your urge for release and response is not as predominant as your need for the clear expression of your self as you are. This is a time where, to paraphrase Willie Nelson, you have outlived your "libido." It no longer interferes with your objectives by stealing the energy through the yearnings or insatiable urges that attend the first phase or the longing for recognition or reflection that accompanies the second. In this day and age it might be very difficult to sort this out with all the propaganda we have received from the commercial world that, first, assumes that everyone at this age has the same intensity of libidinal urgency of their younger years and, second, projects an image that insists that it is "normal" for you to *be* as fit and desirable as you were in your teens and twenties. To add insult to injury, if you're not, it's inferred that there is something wrong with you. To fall for this only says that your comfort with who you are has not reached the fullness of maturity and self acceptance and that you will be unable to take the fullest advantage of this phase without the distraction of self validation.

70-73.5 – Fulfillment Phase

Corresponds to:

Full Moon – I Ching "Li" – Third Opposition – Litha – 180 Degrees

This opposition is the most poignant and, probably, the least visible to the observer. It represents your "returns" on the third time you have *actively* put energy out into the world as a *tangible* attempt to generate healing, teaching and guidance for yourself and others. Your progressed Moon has been reflecting your changing perspective of how you *feel* about the world and its response to your efforts. Transiting Saturn and the progressing Moon in concert have been, hopefully, contributing to your wisdom in understanding the consequences of your personally generated causes and effects. It also makes you painfully aware of how your juniors *don't* understand the consequences of their actions. You know that to confront them with what you see will not only generate a resistive or rebellious reaction in order to save face but it may, in the long run, intensify the consequences generated by their original actions. In a younger time your perspective would have been to prevent them from making the same mistakes as you did in an attempt to spare them the agony of misunderstanding the future consequences. However, in doing so, you may become the enemy. But now, at this age, you've come to realize that experience is the best teacher and that it is *necessary* for them to develop the wisdom, even though it breaks your heart to see them go through the same pain and turmoil as you did. To quote an old adage, "We learn from our failures not from our successes."

In the first two *Fulfillment* phases your largest difficulty was learning to let go of the momentum generated in the preceding fourteen year periods. However, at this age the quality of *what you create* is much more important than the *necessity to create it*. So, in this light, there will be much less personally generated momentum to let go of than was generated in the first two periods. Additionally, you have much more interest in *how* and *where* it will be applied, thereby, lending itself, even more, toward the upcoming *Synthesis* phase than the prior two. With less of an outer directed push of energy to contend with, it is easier to assess your creation more thoroughly. You can see the possible applications even before you have ventured into the upcoming phase and are already calculating how the results will be disseminated. Conversely, if you have not become more content or accepting of your "lot in life," the effects of his whole period of "assessing without possessing" may be mitigated by your goals that have *not* been realized. In this event you will be much more likely to hold on past the time of intended completion if you feel that there is still a chance of realizing their manifestation. Here a proficient assessment is *more* necessary than if you *were* successful in order to understand why you may have missed the mark and to convince you of the necessity to *still* let go. At this age you, hopefully, have realized that all events ebb and flow and that you are willing to go with the Tao (natural flow) of things. The hardest part is to recognize when the tide has turned.

73.5-77 – Synthesis Phase

Corresponds to:

Disseminating Moon – I Ching "K'un" – Third Closing Sesquiquadrate – Lughnasad – 135 Degrees

Most of the creative projects that you have pursued up to this point have been, generally, worldly in nature. As age advances though, thoughts of your mortality enter into your thoughts more often than in younger years. Since the synthesis is about blending your accomplishments back into the flow so as to make things easier for all concerned, that blending becomes more focused on what your family and heritage will take away from you when you've gone. The nurturance of others takes on a whole new perspective. The blending now takes the form of material support as well as any passed on wisdom. Wills are written. Possessions are bequeathed. Business assets and controls are transferred. And the final destination of your assets and wares are determined. This is a time for watching lifetime plans, finally, fall into place.

For those of you who, at this age, have not yet acquired the peace and the contentment that you feel you should have, this "passing on the torch" will be much harder to accomplish. There will be mixed emotions about what to pass on and what not to. There may also be some "waffling" about your feelings since you are not clear on what to do to feel better about your doubtful life perspective. In this case you feel that you want to support your family in their future endeavors but not at the expense of your own support and well being. In analogy, remember the symbolism of the cow and its correspondence to nurturance in earlier discussions. The feeling is much like a new mother who has not yet determined who she is or what she wants before bearing children. There is hesitation for giving full support to her children as the result of a nagging feeling that she has missed something in life potential before the arrival of her family. If you are still attempting to figure out what else must be done, your focus is split and you cannot be receptive to the needs of whom you want to serve as is required by this phase. In this light, giving 98% is *much* harder than giving 100%.

77-80.5 – Reorientation Phase

Corresponds to:

Third Quarter Moon – I Ching "Tui" – Third Closing Square – Mabon – 90 Degrees

After establishing the future distribution and dissemination of your assets and possessions you should be left with a clear field to operate from in determining where and how to focus the remainder of your life which you are aware of as becoming shorter and shorter. In the *reorientation* phase in the first two cycles what you were reorienting *to* was, probably, fairly clear since you still had tangible worldly goals in mind. This third time is a bit different. There may be some tangible goals that you have in mind but also included in the mix is the unknown quality of life you will, or hope to, encounter after life here. I'm not inferring that after the third *release* phase that you will be dying, however, the potential for that is much more likely than after the first two *release* phases. Mortality is becoming a much more dominant theme and the necessity to examine it is more of an issue for you now. Most religions have a much more appealing vision of "rewards and safety" in the afterlife than in lifestyles without. It's more likely, now, that you will move toward religion since it offers the only "plans" of how things are supposed to be after the transition rather than "when you are dead, you're dead." In addition to the task of attempting to solidify your belief system, you find that one of the only places for that type of "information" is through religion. What's distressing about modern day religion is the necessity of separating the material used for manipulation for power by religious pontificates from the material presented by others with only the intention of educating. In this case trust and intuition really get a workout and, hence, all your work and deciding must be done internally. The reorientation here develops a much stronger flavor in learning to trust in the unknown rather than trusting in the effective implementation of a future tangible, partially known, project. Your focus is moving further and further from the material world and more and more into the spirit (energy) world. Unless you have had a direct religious or spiritual experience yourself, the only verification of the professed afterlife that can be acquired is usually based on the hearsay of others, and generally, that falls back to scripture whose interpretation is, often, entirely ambiguous. You're on your own.

Everything thus far has been geared toward dealing with reorienting yourself to the issue of our mortality. What if you are unable to face it? To start with, the process will, probably, have been halted in the *synthesis* phase, if not before. This will show itself in your inability to pass on your creations to the younger generation or even talk about it. Proceeding this time there has been quite a bit of life experience and there may be many strategies utilized in its avoidance. You may be in denial, changing the subject when it arises, arguing about "control" issues, making a joke of it, manifesting an illness such as dementia and other ways of distracting from the focus. Generally, the people comfortable with it generate a calmness about its advance as opposed to a marked nervousness and sense of urgency emanated by those who haven't. Perhaps a religious perspective is one of the only ways to cope with the fear of the oncoming unknown. Only time will tell.

80.5-84 – Release Phase

Corresponds to:

Balsamic Moon – I Ching "Ch'ien" – Third Closing Semisquare – Samhain – 45 Degrees

Probably the best analogy I can make about this phase is you being in mid flight, standing at an open airplane exit, being next in line to perform your first skydive. There is such a mix of excitement and fear (there's no difference between the two in the pit of your stomach except for your attitude; toward or away?) With that jump everything is left behind except what you came in with. The old adage "you can't take it with you" has full impact. This is a time where you find a home for everything you consider of value and let go of the rest. This not only pertains to your possessions but your connection to people and pets. It's like a going out of business clearance sale; everything must go. The letting go of this third *release* phase has much more of an impact and pervasiveness than the prior two cycles. Probably, the most poignant surprise for most is the amount of energy that becomes available upon the letting go. This phase, undoubtedly, frees the most. The only other experience that might compare is the anticipation of coming into life. Yet, in that experience, you are much more aware of what you will be encountering. Upon arriving, your following years find you submitting to training your awareness to only focus on what's necessary for existence in the physical world overshadowing any intangible awareness of where you've come from. Leaving now becomes totally unknown and can only be speculated. Even in this third cycle, and true to the form of the phase, the feeling is *still* one of preparing. For what, you don't know, but preparing nevertheless.

A core issue concerning mortality in this phase is the submission to the possibility of oblivion. This may be conscious or unconscious depending on your awareness and your willingness and ability to consider the concept. Everyone will be different in their methods of dealing with their issues. There is a precarious mixture of experience with belief, desire, self-concept, acceptance, awareness and emotional maturity, just to name a few. The "unanswerable questions" hold a tremendous influence over the resulting perspective. How you handle it is probably the biggest question mark.

CYCLE IV:
ANOTHER DANCE?

84-87.5 – Emergence Phase

Corresponds to:

New Moon – I Ching "K'an" – Third Return – Yule – 000 Degrees

This cycle is a landmark. It *begins* another three part set of cycles at eighty four. Aside from the miracle of the first phase of the first cycle this is probably the most remarkable. This is truly the beginning of your second childhood. It's the only point that you can see a lifetime's full cycle. If your health is good, at this point, it can be the beginning of a brand new adventure. If your life has been allowed to proceed according to natural evolution, its representative is truly the "master" side of the tarot card the Fool or key twenty two. The assumption is that you have evolved a certain brand of wisdom. For some of you, this is so. You have generally learned and know how life is and have learned how to deal with the rest of us who are still learning. You view some of these travelers much like Gandalf the wizard with all his wisdom, compassion, patience and humor. You souls who are gifted in this way are few and far between and a joy to behold when we find you. However, usually found are you folks who are still on the road to growth and appearing to the younger generations as cantankerous, stubborn, childlike (not usually childish), knowing exactly what you want and how everyone else is supposed to behave. Your life determination is what has carried you to this point. To you, others are, at best, inexperienced observers and are often found to be, generally, in the way of what you are attempting to accomplish except for your need of their flexibility and gopher (go for) quality. You usually have a harmless and marked sense of entitlement feeling that you have experienced and "earned" the right of the younger generation's subservience. You have a curious mix of childlike awe when dealing with new experiences and a downright authoritarian attitude when observing others in the process of making a major life faux pas. Having only had minor experience of this nature when dealing with precocious children I can only imagine what is happening psychologically and emotionally in your world. I guess I'll know when and if I arrive there.

45 DEGREE CHART

(Continued on next page)

01 Aries	16 Taurus	01 Cancer	16 Leo	01 Libra	16 Scorpio	01 Capric	16 Aquar
02 Aries	17 Taurus	02 Cancer	17 Leo	02 Libra	17 Scorpio	02 Capric	17 Aquar
03 Aries	18 Taurus	03 Cancer	18 Leo	03 Libra	18 Scorpio	03 Capric	18 Aquar
04 Aries	19 Taurus	04 Cancer	19 Leo	04 Libra	19 Scorpio	04 Capric	19 Aquar
05 Aries	20 Taurus	05 Cancer	20 Leo	05 Libra	20 Scorpio	05 Capric	20 Aquar
06 Aries	21 Taurus	06 Cancer	21 Leo	06 Libra	21 Scorpio	06 Capric	21 Aquar
07 Aries	22 Taurus	07 Cancer	22 Leo	07 Libra	22 Scorpio	07 Capric	22 Aquar
08 Aries	23 Taurus	08 Cancer	23 Leo	08 Libra	23 Scorpio	08 Capric	23 Aquar
09 Aries	24 Taurus	09 Cancer	24 Leo	09 Libra	24 Scorpio	09 Capric	24 Aquar
10 Aries	25 Taurus	10 Cancer	25 Leo	10 Libra	25 Scorpio	10 Capric	25 Aquar
11 Aries	26 Taurus	11 Cancer	26 Leo	11 Libra	26 Scorpio	11 Capric	26 Aquar
12 Aries	27 Taurus	12 Cancer	27 Leo	12 Libra	27 Scorpio	12 Capric	27 Aquar
13 Aries	28 Taurus	13 Cancer	28 Leo	13 Libra	28 Scorpio	13 Capric	28 Aquar
14 Aries	29 Taurus	14 Cancer	29 Leo	14 Libra	29 Scorpio	14 Capric	29 Aquar
15 Aries	00 Gemini	15 Cancer	00 Virgo	15 Libra	00 Sagit	15 Capric	00 Pisces
16 Aries	01 Gemini	16 Cancer	01 Virgo	16 Libra	01 Sagit	16 Capric	01 Pisces
17 Aries	02 Gemini	17 Cancer	02 Virgo	17 Libra	02 Sagit	17 Capric	02 Pisces
18 Aries	03 Gemini	18 Cancer	03 Virgo	18 Libra	03 Sagit	18 Capric	03 Pisces
19 Aries	04 Gemini	19 Cancer	04 Virgo	19 Libra	04 Sagit	19 Capric	04 Pisces
20 Aries	05 Gemini	20 Cancer	05 Virgo	20 Libra	05 Sagit	20 Capric	05 Pisces
21 Aries	06 Gemini	21 Cancer	06 Virgo	21 Libra	06 Sagit	21 Capric	06 Pisces
22 Aries	07 Gemini	22 Cancer	07 Virgo	22 Libra	07 Sagit	22 Capric	07 Pisces
23 Aries	08 Gemini	23 Cancer	08 Virgo	23 Libra	08 Sagit	23 Capric	08 Pisces
24 Aries	09 Gemini	24 Cancer	09 Virgo	24 Libra	09 Sagit	24 Capric	09 Pisces
25 Aries	10 Gemini	25 Cancer	10 Virgo	25 Libra	10 Sagit	25 Capric	10 Pisces
26 Aries	11 Gemini	26 Cancer	11 Virgo	26 Libra	11 Sagit	26 Capric	11 Pisces
27 Aries	12 Gemini	27 Cancer	12 Virgo	27 Libra	12 Sagit	27 Capric	12 Pisces
28 Aries	13 Gemini	28 Cancer	13 Virgo	28 Libra	13 Sagit	28 Capric	13 Pisces
29 Aries	14 Gemini	29 Cancer	14 Virgo	29 Libra	14 Sagit	29 Capric	14 Pisces
00 Taurus	15 Gemini	00 Leo	15 Virgo	00 Scorpio	15 Sagit	00 Aquar	15 Pisces
01 Taurus	16 Gemini	01 Leo	16 Virgo	01 Scorpio	16 Sagit	01 Aquar	16 Pisces
02 Taurus	17 Gemini	02 Leo	17 Virgo	02 Scorpio	17 Sagit	02 Aquar	17 Pisces
03 Taurus	18 Gemini	03 Leo	18 Virgo	03 Scorpio	18 Sagit	03 Aquar	18 Pisces

04 Taurus	19 Gemini	04 Leo	19 Virgo	04 Scorpio	19 Sagit	04 Aquar	19 Pisces
05 Taurus	20 Gemini	05 Leo	20 Virgo	05 Scorpio	20 Sagit	05 Aquar	20 Pisces
06 Taurus	21 Gemini	06 Leo	21 Virgo	06 Scorpio	21 Sagit	06 Aquar	21 Pisces
07 Taurus	22 Gemini	07 Leo	22 Virgo	07 Scorpio	22 Sagit	07 Aquar	22 Pisces
08 Taurus	23 Gemini	08 Leo	23 Virgo	08 Scorpio	23 Sagit	08 Aquar	23 Pisces
09 Taurus	24 Gemini	09 Leo	24 Virgo	09 Scorpio	24 Sagit	09 Aquar	24 Pisces
10 Taurus	25 Gemini	10 Leo	25 Virgo	10 Scorpio	25 Sagit	10 Aquar	25 Pisces
11 Taurus	26 Gemini	11 Leo	26 Virgo	11 Scorpio	26 Sagit	11 Aquar	26 Pisces
12 Taurus	27 Gemini	12 Leo	27 Virgo	12 Scorpio	27 Sagit	12 Aquar	27 Pisces
13 Taurus	28 Gemini	13 Leo	28 Virgo	13 Scorpio	28 Sagit	13 Aquar	28 Pisces
14 Taurus	29 Gemini	14 Leo	29 Virgo	14 Scorpio	29 Sagit	14 Aquar	29 Pisces
15 Taurus	00 Cancer	15 Leo	00 Libra	15 Scorpio	00 Capric	15 Aquar	00 Aries

As an example, let's start with a natal position for transiting Saturn of five degrees of Cancer. This will be the *Emergence* phase. To find the *Assertion* phase just look to the right to twenty degrees of Leo. Each move to the right is forty five degrees equaling one phase. Follow through phase by phase until you have all the points. When you move on from twenty degrees of Aquarius simply wrap around on the other side of the chart with five degrees of Aries for the *Reorientation* phase and continue until you have all the phases. Your completed chart should look like the one to the left.

With these points determined we can now look up the dates for each time transiting Saturn contacts these points. This will give us the personal calendar of change points for the client with natal Saturn at five degrees of Cancer.

You may find the phase positions of any planet starting from its natal position and following the chart in the same manor.

RECOMMENDED READING

A Vision – William Butler Yeats

Astrologer's Handbook – Frances Sakoian & Louis Acker

Concept of Cycle – Charles M Graham

Evolution Through the Tarot – Richard Gardner

I-Ching Workbook – R.L. Wing

I-Ching or Book of Changes – Richard Wilhelm

Inner Structure of the I-Ching – Lama Anagarika Govinda

Lunar Astrology – Alexandre Volguine

Lunation Cycle – Dane Rudhyar

Moon Book – Kim Long

Passages – Gail Sheehy

Planets in Transit – Robert Hand

ABOUT the AUTHOR

John Lawrence Maerz is a philosopher, teacher, artist, musician, massage therapist and self taught astrologer who has been involved in esoteric study since 1966. He is the owner and co-founder of the Astrological Institute of Integrated Studies, Inc. (AIIS) in Margate, Florida which edits and publishes CDs, tapes and books on esoteric studies. He is, also, a former owner and co-founder of Starchild Books in Port Charlotte, Florida. The Astrological Institute was where John Edward received training in Psychic Development, Tarot and Numerology from John Maerz and his former business partner, Sandy Anastasi, in the mid eighties which was, then, in Bayshore, NY. Starchild Books is among the first places that John Edward held "gallery" sessions before the release of the book "One Last Time" and the airing of "Crossing Over" on the SciFi network.

John's four year degree in Psychology and Education from C.W. Post College in New York paved the way for offering life insights and career counseling through private sessions and in his newsletter, "The Rising Star."

As a teacher John's experience extends to many metaphysical areas as well. He began teaching himself astrology in 1966. Astrology then led to Numerology, Tarot, Kabbala, I-Ching, Tai Chi and Chi Kung. As a result of having had the honor to sponsor John Edward in the late nineties he was inspired to help construct a curriculum for the developing of Spirit Communication abilities in the students who passed through AIIS and Starchild. Besides his work as a teacher John M., is, also, an effective medium and occasionally conducts gallery style "messages" sessions himself.

As an advisor John is a professional coach and has a diverse background in the human potentials field incorporating personality influences, shadow work, nutritional needs, creative expression and personal desires while uncovering innate abilities and hidden potentials for his clients. He is dedicated toward raising awareness and shares his own unique understandings and perspectives about life's journey and meaning. He, also, recognizes the need for balance and accountability on our mental, physical and emotional levels as well as fulfilling our spiritual potential through individual experience.

As a holistic healer John primarily focuses on moving energy throughout his patient's body to release blockages. He specializes in Shiatsu, Cranial Sacral work, energy work, including Reiki, and is well versed in diet and nutrition as well. He's been a vegetarian for over 30 years and is a student of Eastern Medicine and Herbology. As a Reiki Master Healer, John periodically offers classes teaching Reiki.

Prior to opening the Astrological Institute of Integrated Studies (1983) and Starchild New Age Books & Gifts (1995), John's life and career were diverse. He's worked on an aircraft carrier flight deck (four years), in retail hardware (thirteen years), electronics (six years), youth counseling (two years) and in other New Age stores (fifteen years). He has been on both radio and TV in New York and Florida and is proud to have been one of the teachers involved in John Edward's meteoric rise to fame.

John currently lives and works in Margate, Florida.